THE EXPRESS

THE CLEVER
COOKBOOK

ORLANDO MURRIN

Illustrations by Helen J Holroyd

Foreword by Robert Carrier

SIMON & SCHUSTER
A VIACOM COMPANY

First published in Great Britain by Simon & Schuster UK Ltd, 1999
A Viacom Company

1 3 5 7 9 10 8 6 4 2

Simon & Schuster UK Ltd
Africa House
64-78 Kingsway
London WC2B 6AH

Design: Jane Humphrey
Typeset by Stylize Digital Artwork
Printed in Hong Kong

A CIP catalogue record for this book is available from the British Library

ISBN 0 684 85846 0

For David

Contents

Foreword

It has never ceased to astound me that energetic, busy men like Orlando Murrin can find time to cook and entertain, (after all this man is the editor of *BBC Good Food* magazine, writes the Clever Cook column for *The Express*, and in his carefree playtime is the romping, raging pianist at the Pizza Express). Yet he still manages to give sumptuous weekend parties at his country home in Oxfordshire with caviar and blinis, Roman lamb (slow braised with rosemary) and the best chocolate cake I have ever tasted. I know: I was there. As were the magazine guru Liz Glaze, sculptor Maggi Hambling and painter Lady Oaksey. It all ended up with us cavorting and singing lusty songs around the piano, with Orlando at the keyboard, until 3.30 am.

Orlando is the most relaxed, genial, charming and down-to-earth food writer you could wish for. He is one of those superbly creative cooks who, given four lamb chops, a packet of curry leaves and a few new potatoes at the back of the larder, can turn out a wonderfully exotic oven roast with Asian overtones, sauced with a ginger- and garlic-flavoured papaya purée. Quick, economical, different – and a blaze of flavours. That's the kind of impromptu cooking I love, and which home cooks dream about.

The hallmark of Orlando's busy life is the constant drive for change, for new challenges, for excellence. This flamboyant food impresario has come a long way since his first timid food presentation on Loyd Grossman's *MasterChef*. He won through to the semi-finals, even though he had never watched the programme. It was immediately evident that he has a particular skill – so right for today's fast-lane living – the ability to combine flavours and textures to make a perfect meal, under pressure, in a matter of minutes.

Followers of Orlando's Clever Cook column who have been carefully saving tattered clippings for the past two years, can now throw their hoard away, safe in the knowledge that this brilliant, easy-to-use cookbook is right by the cooker, ready to pull out and cook Cinderella Potatoes, Roquefort Quiche, Slow Roast Belly of Pork, Irish Potato Cakes, Nectarines in Mascarpone and Pear Tarte Tatin.

Orlando knows that interesting food can act as a conversation stimulus. His motto is: "Don't be afraid to experiment" and this book is the result of inspired experimentation over the years. Simply delicious.

Orlando's credo

- Regard cooking as a pleasure, not a chore.
- Always use fresh, good-quality produce.
- Taste as you go along. Nothing ever tastes the same as the last time you cooked it.
- Always undercook (just a little) to spotlight the intrinsic texture and flavour of the ingredients.
- Make your food look delicious as well as taste delicious.
- Always have really hot plates for hot food and really cold plates for chilled soups and salads.
- Keep it simple. Simplicity is the most important ingredient of all.

Robert Carrier

Acknowledgements

Clever Cook would never have happened without Richard Addis taking a gamble; I would like to thank Rosie Boycott, the Express Editor, for her continued support and encouragement.

Helen Holroyd is the most talented and amenable of illustrators, and takes endless trouble to ensure her pictures are helpful to the cook, as well as beautiful to look at.

Recipe development depends on teamwork. My mother is my official tester, my father quality controller: I would like to thank them for their patience, diligence and good humour. Life in the kitchen would be intolerable without the kindness of David Manson, who also does most of the shopping, and Mrs Coleman, our civilising influence. I would be lost without my butcher, Pat Thomas of Faringdon, Oxfordshire, and I would like to thank my fishmonger, Mr Page – just retired – for his help over several years.

At *The Express*, I am indebted to my editors, Nigel Billen, Jackie Holland and Bronwen Holly, plus Sally, Jocelyn, Mary and Jo Dimond behind the scenes. The idea for the book came from Sue McGeever and Mark Burgess. My column has been steered by the comments, compliments (and criticism) of a voluminous postbag; thank you to *Express* readers who wrote in.

At *BBC Good Food* magazine, I would like to thank Mary Cadogan, Angela Nilsen, Nicola Kelly, Siobhan Keeler, Lynne Stanford and Vivien Bowler for advice and practical help.

Many of the recipes in this book have been contributed by, or adapted from, recipes of friends, readers and other cookery writers. On this score I would specially like to thank Brian and Sheila Ketterer, Carol Bronze, Elizabeth Mackenzie, Franco Taruschio, Gina Marreco, Jean Manson, Joan Coleman, Lavinia Hankinson, Martha Hare, Martina Langer, Patricia Gregory, Peter Gordon, Vera Bainville, Shona Crawford Poole, Robert Carrier, Stephen Mudge, Susanna Gelmetti, Lindsey Bareham, Diana Gordon, Francis Emmorey, Pat Holness, Susie Fairfax, Patricia Gregory, Lady Hornby, Jacqueline Lewin, Liz Glaze, Bryony Fuller, Anni Bowes, Meriel Greenwood, Susan Gough and Susannah Mudge.

Introduction

I am the world's greatest fan of home cooking. Give me the choice between whisking something up in the kitchen and going out to a Michelin-starred restaurant, and – not always, but 9 times out of 10 – I would rather be at home.

With home cooking you know exactly what you're eating and you can customise it to your own taste. What's more it's incredibly relaxing, as creative as you want it to be, and gives you a warm glow of satisfaction when you eat the results.

The one thing all these recipes have in common is their practicality. I love spending time in the kitchen, but I hate wasting it. Everything has been personally cooked and tasted by me; and if an early attempt ended up with a mountain of washing up, or bits of packets left over, or that feeling that I'd been beating round the bush, I've re-organised the recipe so the same fate doesn't happen to you. That's not to say that every dish in the book is quick and easy – but I hope at least everything is enjoyable to make. If you've a better way of doing something, please let me know for next time.

Something else that will immediately declare itself to the reader is that my food is essentially British, based on familiar ingredients, techniques and combinations. I enjoy exotic food and marvel at the range of ingredients you can readily buy, but at heart I am a traditionalist. I love finding an old, perhaps forgotten dish, and recreating it for modern tastes. Or making something new and different out of ingredients you will find in any storecupboard throughout the land.

Starters and salads

The dividing line between a starter and a light main course is a slender one, especially in the warmer months of the year, and almost all these recipes will fit in with your wishes. Most also have the advantage that you can make them in advance – essential in my opinion if you are entertaining.

You will find several salads – hot, warm and cold – in this chapter, and I find them a particularly rewarding sort of cooking; they invite you to be creative and experimental but you know that you're going to have something good to eat at the end.

This is an impressive salad invented by my friends Brian and Sheila who live in Newbury. Castle Cottage is well known locally for many things, not least its thriving tortoise colony. One of the finest summer experiences must be to enjoy this main course salad in their enchanting, flower-filled garden, with the herbs freshly plucked from the vegetable patch.

Castle cottage salad

- Easy
- No cooking required
- 20 minutes to assemble
Serves: 4–6

500g/1lb 2oz smoked chicken, or skinned, boned, cooked chicken
2 sticks of celery
1 lettuce
50g/2oz pack of roast salted peanuts
2 crisp eating apples
handful of chopped herbs (chives, tarragon, lovage – whatever the tortoises don't eat)
salt and pepper

For the Dressing
small carton of plain thick yogurt
4 tbsp olive oil
4 tbsp orange juice
1 tsp paprika
dash of Tabasco, optional
pinch of sugar

Experiment with your favourite garden herbs for this salad.

1. Skin and shred the flesh of the smoked chicken or shred the chicken. Slice the celery and lettuce and put in a bowl with the peanuts. Refrigerate if you go thus far in advance.

2. Whisk the dressing ingredients with salt and pepper.

3. Just before serving, peel and slice the apples thinly and chop the herbs (see below). Toss everything together and serve.

Tip 1: *Look out for smoked chicken in good delicatessens, smoked food specialists and Waitrose.*

Tip 2: *Different herbs are best handled as follows. Parsley, lovage, oregano, marjoram and mint: chop as finely as possible (be patient) for best flavour. Chives: snip finely as large pieces catch in your teeth. Tarragon and chervil: don't chop too finely or the flavour evaporates before you eat it. Rosemary, thyme and sage: best used to flavour foods during cooking, in which case use whole sprigs and leaves. Basil: cut or tear into pieces about 1cm (½ inch) across at the very last minute (flavour evaporates quickly). Sorrel: if cooking, it melts almost instantly to a sludge, so simply remove stems, don't chop; if adding to a salad, use as basil (but go easy as it's rather sour).*

This recipe is a present to us all from a fantastic cook, Elizabeth Mackenzie. Readers in the isle of Mull may remember Elizabeth as the gardener who transformed Calgary Castle into a Himalayan paradise.

In the kitchen Elizabeth had an equally magic touch, and introduced me to such ethereal delights as blackcurrant leaf ice. This is one of her signature first courses.

1. Sprinkle the aspic powder over 300ml/½ pint hot water in a small pan and heat until it has dissolved and becomes clear – you will need to bring it just to the boil (but don't worry if it does come to the boil, it won't be spoilt). You now need to cool it; if in a hurry you can put the pan in a larger bowl full of iced water, otherwise leave for 45 minutes until cold enough to put in the fridge, then about 30 minutes in the fridge, the object being to get the aspic thoroughly cold and on the point of setting. If you miss your moment and it actually sets, just heat it for a second to liquify it again.
2. Meanwhile, whip the cream lightly, and in another bowl, whip the egg whites till stiff. Take a large bowl and put in the aspic, whipped cream and egg whites, cheese and cayenne, and fold all together thoroughly. Turn into a 1.2 litre/2 pint capacity soufflé dish and chill for 3–24 hours. Dust lightly with paprika before serving.

Tip: *Although it sounds so old-fashioned, aspic is fun and easy to use. But where supermarkets choose to put it is a fascinating mystery: I discovered it on a shelf above the cooked meats in Sainsbury's – most imaginative.*

One of the most elegant summer starters imaginable

Chilled parmesan soufflé

- Fun to make
- 15 minutes actual cooking
- 3-24 hours chilling
Serves: 6
- Best made the day before

half a 25g/1oz sachet of aspic
    powder
284ml carton of double cream
2 egg whites
50g/2oz freshly grated
    parmesan cheese
cayenne pepper
a little paprika
toast, to serve

A flavourful chicken concoction on a Far Eastern theme

Chinese chicken and aubergine salad

- Not difficult
- 30 minutes to prepare
- 1¼ hours cooking

Serves: 6–8

650g/1½ lb aubergines
a little peanut or sunflower oil
1.8kg/4lb chicken
1 tbsp sesame seeds

For the Basting Mixture
1 tbsp soy sauce
2 tbsp black treacle
1 tsp toasted sesame oil

For the Dressing
2.5cm/1-inch cube of ginger, grated (no need to peel)
3 cloves of garlic, roughly chopped
1 red or green chilli, seeded and roughly chopped
5 tbsp rice or cider vinegar
5 tbsp soy sauce
1 tsp toasted sesame oil
3 tbsp peanut or sunflower oil

To Finish
pack of fresh coriander
6 spring onions

This is a most elegant and unusual starter.

1. Preheat oven to 220°C/fan oven 200°C/gas 7. Slice the aubergines into thin rounds, about 5mm/¼-inch thick. Line a large baking sheet with foil or baking paper, put them on it in one layer and sprinkle with salt, pepper and a little oil. Put the chicken in a roasting pan and the sesame seeds in a small ovenproof dish or tin, and put all three in the oven.

2. Toast the sesame seeds for 5–10 minutes, until slightly darkened. Roast the aubergines for 10–15 minutes, turning once, until tender to the point of a knife. Allow to cool. Mix together the ingredients for the basting mixture. After 15 minutes, remove chicken from oven and baste all over with the basting mixture. Turn the oven down to 170°C/fan oven 150°C/gas 4 and roast for a further hour, adding a cup of boiling water when the basting mixture looks dry (see tip) and basting frequently. Set aside to cool.

3. Whizz the first five ingredients of the dressing in a blender till smooth, then add the oils and whizz again. The dressing can be made in advance.

4. To assemble the salad, skin and bone the chicken and tear the flesh into strips. Halve the aubergine slices. Chop half the coriander and slice the spring onions thinly on the diagonal. Just before serving, mix everything together with the dressing, check seasoning, then top with the whole coriander leaves and the toasted sesame seeds.

Tip: *The basting mixture rapidly dries out and you will need to add a little water about four times in all.*

Every summer we have a guess-the-weight-of-the-pumpkin competition in my garden. The most ingenious attempt involved my godson Matthew rolling himself into a pumpkin shape and being lifted up by his brother to see if he outweighed the prize vegetable.

I've always found pumpkin soup rather bland, but this version is full of flavour and character.

1. In the processor, chop the garlic and chilli very finely. Add the onion and celery and chop. Or do this by hand – washing hands after touching the chilli.
2. In a large casserole with a lid, heat the oil. Add the chopped mixture, and sweat with the lid on, over a moderate heat, for 5 minutes. Add the curry paste or powder and continue for another 5 minutes. The vegetables will be softened but not brown.
3. Meanwhile, cut the skin off the pumpkin (with care – they're lethally slippery) and scrape out seeds and fibre with a metal spoon. Cut into rough 2cm/1-inch chunks. Pour boiling water over tomatoes, then skin, seed and cut them up (this is not necessary if you are using a mouli in step 5, as the mouli will remove them for you).
4. Add tomatoes and pumpkin to the pan with the stock and saffron. Bring to the boil and simmer for 20 minutes, covered.
5. Check the pumpkin is soft, then either put the soup through a mouli, or process until smooth.
6. Add the coconut milk, heat till boiling and serve.

Tip: *It's not easy to find coconut milk in the supermarket – the curry section is your best bet.*

Curried pumpkin soup

- Easy
- 15 minutes preparation
- 30 minutes cooking
Serves: 6
- Can be made up to step 6 and frozen

1 clove of garlic
1 red chilli
1 onion, preferably red
1 stick of celery
1 tbsp oil
1 tbsp curry paste or 2 tsp powder
one 1.3kg/3lb pumpkin (or 600g/1lb 5oz pumpkin flesh)
2 tomatoes
pinch of saffron, optional
200ml/7fl oz chicken stock
half a 400ml tin of coconut milk

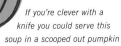

If you're clever with a knife you could serve this soup in a scooped out pumpkin

Hot sausage salad

- Very easy
- 30 minutes in total

Serves: 4

350g/12oz your favourite
    sausages (half a dozen)
450g/1lb potatoes
    (4 medium ones)
3 eggs
1 egg yolk
150ml/¼ pint mayonnaise
juice of half a lemon
1 tbsp grainy mustard
chives
salt and freshly ground black
    pepper

I'm a great fan of sausages, and although I have a sausage-making attachment on my food mixer, you can actually buy better than you can make, in the most outlandish combinations if that's what you fancy.

This is a good honest winter salad, served hot because that's what we need in this damp climate of ours. I say honest, but it carries a strong potential for deceit, as herein I reveal the trick of making bought mayonnaise indistinguishable from home-made.

All it involves is starting with an egg yolk (if you're concerned about raw egg yolks, this rules you out) and whisking bought mayonnaise into it; you get that subtle egg and olive oil flavour and translucence without that drop-by-drop beating in of the oil.

1. Heat the oven to 150°C/gas 2. Fry the sausages in the usual way, about 10 minutes, then cut into chunks. Meanwhile peel, chunk and boil the potatoes until just tender but not collapsing (about 15 minutes). Hardboil the eggs for 10 minutes, peel and quarter.
2. Put the egg yolk in a large mixing bowl and whisk in the mayonnaise, tablespoon by tablespoon. Check seasoning, grind in some black pepper and beat in the lemon juice and mustard; snip in a good handful of chives.
3. Pile the sausages, potatoes and eggs into the mayonnaise, fold all together gently, transfer to a large serving dish and warm for 10 minutes in the oven. Serve with bread.

Tip: *If serving this for children, add 1 tablespoon of ketchup instead of the mustard.*

A jamboree of satisfyingly familiar ingredients

This is my favourite soup in the world – exceptionally mild and delicate in flavour, with a creamy consistency all its own. It needs no beefing up or embellishment – this very old recipe does the Jerusalem artichoke perfect justice

The knobbly outside of the Jerusalem artichoke conceals a truly princely flavour

Jerusalem artichoke soup

- Easy
- 1 hour 20 minutes in total

Serves: 8

- Makes 2 litres/3½ pints
- Can be prepared ahead or frozen and reheated up to the end of step 2

25g/1lb 12oz butter
2 onions
800g/1lb 12oz Jerusalem
  artichokes (see tip)
600ml/1 pint stock or water
  in which you have boiled
  potatoes
600ml/1 pint milk
pinch of sugar
15g/½oz butter or 2 tbsp
  cream, to finish, optional
salt and white pepper

For the Croûtons
2 thick slices white bread
25g/1oz butter

1. In a generous casserole with a lid, heat the butter. Skin and slice the onions and add. Cover and cook for 5 minutes to sweat – onions should be soft and transparent but in no way brown. Meanwhile, peel the artichokes (I find a swivel potato peeler best for this) and slice, and add to the casserole. Sweat, stirring occasionally, for 15 minutes until just tender when touched with the point of a knife.

2. Pour in the stock or potato water, season with salt, ground white pepper and a good pinch of sugar and simmer for 20 minutes until the artichokes are fully softened. Liquidise in two batches and reheat with the milk.

3. Bring to the boil, stir through the butter (which adds gloss and heightens flavour) or cream. Serve with the croûtons, made by frying the bread, cubed, in the butter for 10 minutes (watch like a hawk and turn frequently) and seasoning generously.

Tip: *If buying Jerusalem artichokes loose, choose ones that aren't too knobbly as they're far easier to peel. If peeling is slow and arduous, drop the peeled artichokes into water acidulated with a tablespoon of lemon juice to stop them going brown. If you wish, one drop (only) of green food colouring will give this soup an enchanting eau de nil colour, though this isn't strictly necessary.*

Martha's salad

- Very easy
- 15 minutes to prepare
- 5 minutes to brown nuts

Serves: 6

50g/2oz unsalted macadamia
    nuts
250g/9oz cooked, shelled
    tiger prawns
1 spring onion
3 ripe avocados
paprika, for serving

For the Dressing
4 tbsp mayonnaise
2 tbsp plain yogurt
1 tbsp lemon juice
2 tsp ketchup
1 tbsp syrup from a jar of
    stem ginger
splash of Worcestershire sauce
seasoning

*A beautiful exotic nut
to look out for*

I was first introduced to macadamia nuts through the novels of John Updike, whose hero (known as Rabbit) munches them much as you or I might turn to chocolate. They are rather like large hazelnuts, only slightly softer to the bite, and very rich indeed.

My friend Martha Hare recently visited from New York, where macadamias are a trendy ingredient. She explained that they originate in Hawaii, and that they have a natural affinity with avocado. Here is a salad dedicated to Martha. If you can't find macadamias – and they are currently only stocked by good health food shops and very large supermarkets – use skinned hazelnuts instead. If you can only find salted macadamias, rinse the salt off before toasting, and if you can only find salted roasted ones, simply rinse and dry well before using.

1. Preheat oven to 200°C/fan oven 180°C/gas 6 and toast the macadamia nuts for 5 minutes, rolling them in the pan once or twice but watch carefully. Slice them roughly. Dry the prawns. Shred the spring onion.
2. Make the dressing by whisking together all the dressing ingredients – it will be a very pale pink.
3. Just before serving, halve the avocados (best done by slicing then twisting the two halves apart), remove stone by tomahawking it with your knife then twisting out, peel off skin and cut into largish chunks. Put in a bowl with the nuts, prawns and spring onion. Arrange decoratively in a shallow bowl, pour over the dressing and dust with paprika to serve.

Tip: *Some supermarkets now do brilliant "ripe and ready to eat" avocados which take the guesswork out of choosing.*

I just love this simple Italian starter. Its origins lie in a wonderful recipe book called *Leaves from the Walnut Tree*, by Ann and Franco Taruschio. The Walnut Tree is their restaurant near Abergavenny which I have on my list of must-visits.

I once gave a rather unnerving dinner for a group of food writers and experts, and this is the first course I chose. It improves by being made well in advance, and the flavours are simply wonderful.

1. Preheat oven to 190°C/fan oven 170°C/gas 5. Halve the peppers and under running water remove stems, cores and seeds. Leave to drain.

2. Drain the tomatoes in a sieve (save juices for another recipe – you will have about 300ml/½ pint) and halve roughly. Drain the anchovies and halve lengthwise. Chop the garlic finely.

3. Put the peppers in a large roasting dish, cut sides up. Put a couple of tomato halves in each pepper, topped with a couple of strips of anchovy. Dot with the garlic and some freshly ground black pepper, then drizzle olive oil over all.

4. Bake for 40 minutes, until beginning to soften. At the Walnut Tree they suggest 20 minutes, but I prefer my peppers slightly softer. Serve hot or cold with good bread.

Tip: *The original recipe calls for fresh plum tomatoes, but I find that tinned tomatoes have a flavour and richness that you can't get from fresh, except in midsummer. As tinned tomatoes come from Italy in the first place, I have a feeling Franco and Ann will support me in this.*

Your kitchen will be filled with the aroma of Italy

Piedmontese peppers

- Easy
- 20 minutes to prepare
- 40 minutes to cook

Serves: 6

- Make ahead if convenient (easily adapted to other numbers)

6 peppers – 3 red, 3 yellow
2 × 400g/14oz tins of plum tomatoes (not chopped tomatoes)
50g/2oz tin of anchovy fillets
3 cloves of garlic
125ml/4fl oz extra virgin olive oil
freshly ground black pepper

This simple dish was invented for my father's birthday. Regular readers of the Clever Cook column will know that his input to the recipes is essential: my mother being official double-tester, my father official taster. Everything that goes into the paper has to be given the thumbs-up, and here is a dish made for him: a generous medley of tasty, honest ingredients.

Potato and black pudding salad

- Easy
- 25 minutes from start to finish

Serves: 4 as a main course salad

450g/1lb new potatoes
225g/½lb black pudding (see tip)
2 sticks of celery
1 small red onion
2 tbsp olive oil

For the Dressing
2 tbsp olive oil
1 tsp wine or cider vinegar
1 tsp wholegrain mustard
dash of Tabasco, optional

1. Prepare the potatoes and boil in salted water till tender, about 15–20 minutes. Meanwhile, slice the black pudding into 1cm/½-inch slices, finely slice the celery and chop the onion.

2. Heat the oil in a large frying pan and fry the black pudding, turning once, for 4 minutes. Remove to a piece of kitchen paper. Add the chopped onion and fry for 4 minutes (red onions cook slightly faster than ordinary ones), then add the celery and fry 2 minutes more. Pile on to the kitchen paper with the black pudding.

3. Finally, take the frying pan (no need to rinse or wipe) and add the dressing ingredients off the heat – whisk together, but don't worry if they don't go smooth, this is no problem. Drain the potatoes when done, cut into bite-size pieces, and add to the pan. Quarter the slices of black pudding and add them to the pan with the onion and celery. Turn into a hot serving dish and serve at once, while still warm.

Tip: *Black pudding sometimes seems to be encased in a thick black plasticky skin. I peel this off and throw it away, and sometimes the pudding fries up into weird shapes. This is nothing to worry about – it tastes just as good.*

A stylish lunch dish in black and white

We are lucky to have this exclusive salad, which was the big hit in Monaco a few years back and was smuggled to me by my friend Vera Bainville. Mme Bainville says its inventor was one of France's greatest chefs, Paul Bocuse. Despite this grand provenance it is very little fuss to make, and I invite you to sit back, shut your eyes and think of yachts and sunshine as you savour its piquant flavours and textures.

Stilton is a good alternative to Roquefort, especially if you can only buy those plastic packets of Roquefort, which always seem to be oily when you unwrap them.

1. Slice the walnuts and toast in a 200°C/fan oven 190°C/gas 6 oven for 3–5 minutes – watching like an elkhound as walnuts toast quickly, especially when cut small. Put the leaves in a large glass bowl, chop or crumble the cheese and sprinkle over the leaves. Halve the tomatoes and lay on top and sprinkle over the cooled walnuts. Refrigerate until ready.

2. Make the dressing – this can also be done in advance – by whizzing, shaking in a jar or whisking all ingredients together with 1 tbsp water (to soften the acidity) and seasoning. At the last minute, chop the tarragon leaves finely (discard stalks), sprinkle over the salad, pour over the dressing and toss. Though messy, this is one of those kitchen jobs best done gently with the hands.

Tip: *My correspondent specifies that ideally the salad should comprise three parts of green to one of red salad leaves.*

Slice the walnuts for this salad rather than chopping them

Salade Bainville

- Easy
- No cooking (except toasting the walnuts)
- 15 minutes to prepare

Serves: 4

50–100g/2–4oz walnuts (depends how nutty you like your salads)
2 small (80g) bags of prepared salad leaves (green and red leaves)
85g/3oz Roquefort or Stilton
225g/8oz cherry tomatoes
salt and freshly ground black pepper
large bunch of tarragon, to finish

For the Dressing
1 tbsp tarragon or cider vinegar
4 tbsp olive oil
1 tbsp nut oil, optional
1 tsp Dijon mustard
pinch of sugar

Like many of the best recipes, this extremely British recipe came to me via an American – my New Yorker friend Carol Bronze. I'm not sure where she found it, but I suspect it was this side of the Atlantic; there are many variants of the recipe floating round, but I think this very simple version the best.

Stilton soup

- Easy
- 45 minutes to prepare and cook

Serves: 4

- Can be prepared up to 24 hours ahead
- Freezes well (do this before adding cream in step 3)

1 leek
1 onion
1 large potato
50g/2oz butter
1 tbsp flour
600ml/1 pint chicken stock
150ml/¼ pint dry cider
300ml/½ pint milk
100g/4oz Stilton
4 tbsp double cream
salt and freshly ground black
    pepper

1. Chop the vegetables finely (this can be done in a food processor). Melt the butter in a large, lidded heavy-bottomed pan and add the vegetables. Cook without browning, with lid on, for 7 minutes, stirring every couple of minutes to hinder sticking.

2. Stir in the flour, then add the stock and cider gradually. Cover and simmer gently for 30 minutes, stirring occasionally – until vegetables are tender.

3. Add milk and Stilton, crumbled, and heat gently until the cheese has melted. Taste and season, then liquidise. Reheat and stir in the cream before serving.

Tip: *Heavy-bottomed pans tend to distribute heat better and burn food less.*

A perfect combination of ingredients

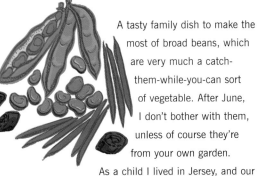

A tasty family dish to make the most of broad beans, which are very much a catch-them-while-you-can sort of vegetable. After June, I don't bother with them, unless of course they're from your own garden.

As a child I lived in Jersey, and our neighbour used to present my mother proudly with home-grown vegetables, which grew like the beanstalk in that sunny, fertile place. Unfortunately he was of the opinion that the bigger the better and no amount of boiling would tenderise some of the beans and peas he gave us. If Mr Coutanche is looking down from that great allotment in the sky, thank you nevertheless for your generosity.

Warm summer bean and sausage salad

- Extremely easy
- 10 minutes to prepare
- 20 minutes to cook

Serves: 4

450g/1lb broad beans
100g/4oz French beans
450g/1lb pork sausages
1 tbsp oil
2 tbsp pesto
handful of parsley, lovage or
   mixed herbs

1. Pod the broad beans and trim the French beans. Put a large pan of salted water on to boil and add the broad beans. After 4 minutes, add the French beans and cook for 4–5 minutes, till both are tender. Drain well.

2. Meanwhile, heat the oil and prick the sausages. Cook in the usual way, until nicely browned (10–12 minutes). Remove the sausages and slice attractively on the diagonal. Wipe the pan with kitchen paper and add the sausages and beans, then stir in the pesto until well combined; warm through. Transfer to a serving dish and sprinkle with finely chopped herbs to bring out the flavour.

Tip: *If you are a broad bean fan, you can peel the pale green covering from each bean to reveal the sweet apple-green mini-bean at the centre. These need no cooking, and are lovely in salads.*

Warm three cheese salad

- Easy
- 20 minutes preparation
Serves: 2
- Double or triple recipe as necessary

For the Croûtons
2 slices of stale bread, crusts removed and cubed
1 clove of garlic, peeled and halved lengthwise
knob of butter
2 tsp olive oil

For the Dressing
2.5cm/1-inch cube of Stilton
juice of ¼ lemon
2 tbsp olive oil
1 tsp Dijon mustard
pinch of sugar
1 tbsp water

For the Salad
70g crisp salad leaves (lettuce, chicory, watercress, spinach)
4 cherry tomatoes
salt and freshly ground black pepper

To Finish
1 × 100g/4oz round of British goats' cheese
mature cheddar cheese
a little extra virgin or walnut oil (optional)

1. Fry the bread gently in the butter and oil with the garlic until golden and crisp – 10–15 minutes. Watch carefully. Season lightly, discard garlic and set to one side.

2. Meanwhile, turn grill to high and make the dressing. Either mash the Stilton and whisk in other ingredients or put them all in the liquidiser and whizz for 10 seconds, or until smooth. Taste carefully as you season – Stilton is salty.

3. In a large bowl, tear up the salad leaves into bite-size pieces. Halve or quarter the tomatoes and toss with the salad leaves.

4. Cut the goats' cheese into six like a cake. Put the segments on a square of foil allowing room for them to melt a little and put under a hot grill for 4–5 minutes until golden.

5. Meanwhile, add the warm croûtons and dressing to the salad and toss. Arrange on individual plates, then, using a palette knife or slice, carefully arrange the goat's cheese on top. Finish with cheddar curls, made by flicking a potato peeler over a block of cheddar – about 10–15 curls per portion – and if you wish a drizzle of oil and plenty of freshly ground pepper.

Tip: *Adding a little water to a vinaigrette dressing delays the sensation of lemon or vinegar on the palate and makes the flavour more rounded and mild, without diluting the flavour.*

Suppers and
main courses

Many of the dishes in this chapter have been created around old favourites, while others are unique and special enough for entertaining.

One of the secrets for making really tasty, satisfying food is long cooking times which enable the flavours to mingle and the meat to cook to almost melting tenderness; such recipes can even save you time, if preparation is minimal and the cooking looks after itself.

I fell in love with pasta when I was three. You will also find several quick and I hope inspiring ideas for pasta in this chapter.

This is the ultimate comfort food, and was inspired by a postcard sent to me signed Joan H of Chester. It begged, "please can we have a recipe for a good old-fashioned bacon and onion roly-poly?" I hope you enjoy this as much as I do. Served with gravy, mash and broccoli you have a meal fit for a king.

This is a brilliantly economical dish, and even if you bought everything at Harrods food halls I doubt you could spend more than £1.20 on the ingredients.

Bacon and onion roly poly

- Fun to make
- 20 minutes to prepare
- 2 hours steaming
Serves: 3–4

2 onions
100g/4oz streaky bacon
oil for frying
salt and freshly ground black
    pepper

For the Suet Crust
100g/4oz suet
85g/3oz breadcrumbs
175g/6oz self-raising flour
100ml/3½fl oz water or milk
+ extra milk for brushing

1. Slice the onions and bacon and fry for 7 minutes till soft and golden. Cool.

2. Get ready a large pan of water that will accommodate a 20cm/8-inch sausage. Bring to the boil. Make the suet crust by mixing the dry ingredients together, seasoning and then mixing in some water or milk to make a stiffish pastry. Roll out on a floured board using a floured rolling pin to a rectangle about 20 × 33cm/ 8 × 13 inches.

3. Spread the onion and bacon mixture over the surface, allowing a 2cm/¾-inch border all the way round. Brush the border with milk and roll up, pressing firmly on all edges to seal.

4. Wrap in baking parchment, crimping edges tightly but allowing room for the roly poly to rise, then wrap twice similarly in foil. Immerse in the pan of boiling water and simmer for 2 hours. Fish out, unwrap and serve in slices with gravy and a green vegetable.

Tip: *After this recipe was published in The Express, a reader wrote and said that a savoury roly-poly is even better if you sprinkle it with dried mixed herbs before rolling and cooking.*

The most tasty and nostalgic supper dish imaginable

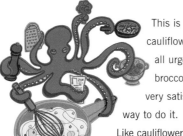

This is a new take on cauliflower cheese. We are all urged to eat more broccoli and this is a very satisfying and tasty way to do it.

Like cauliflower cheese, this is one of those apparently straightforward dishes that requires several cooking operations to proceed simultaneously. This is one of the many times in life I wish I had been born an octopus.

1. Preheat the grill. Put salted water on to boil for the broccoli and trim the florets neatly. Boil for 8 minutes, or until tender. Drain and keep warm.
2. Meanwhile, fry the gammon in the oil for about 5 minutes, until going golden. Set pan and contents aside.
3. Put the spring onions, butter, flour and milk – all cold – into a medium-sized pan (not non-stick). Whisk over a medium heat with a balloon or gravy whisk constantly until it thickens, about 5–6 minutes. Then boil, stirring frequently, for 3 minutes and set aside.
4. Put the broccoli in a wide shallow dish and sprinkle with the gammon and pan juices.
5. Mix ¾ of the cheese and the mustard into the white sauce and season. Pour over the broccoli, sprinkle with the remaining cheese and dot with butter, then grill for just 2 minutes, until golden and bubbling.

Tip: *There seems to be a craze for undercooking broccoli in restaurants, the result being tasteless and indigestible. I agree there is no merit in a slimy green mush either, but if you test carefully it is not hard to achieve something in between that is tender and tasty.*

Whisk the pan constantly and the ingredients will miraculously combine into a smooth white sauce

Broccoli and ham cheese

● Very straightforward
● 30 minutes to prepare and cook
Serves: 4 as a supper or lunch dish
● Not for freezing

900g/2lb broccoli (about 675g/ 1lb 8oz of florets, when trimmed)
200g/8oz smoked gammon steak, cut into matchsticks
1 tbsp oil
3 spring onions, finely chopped
25g/1oz butter
25g/1oz (1 heaped tbsp) plain flour
425ml/¾ pint milk
115g/4oz cheddar, grated
2 tsp mustard
a little butter
salt and freshly ground black pepper

At one time it was necessary to roast a chicken in order to have leftover chicken. Now if you don't have the real thing, there is always cooked chicken to save time and trouble.

This recipe – like many you will find in this book – is an adaptation of a very familiar British favourite, in this case shepherd's pie, but with the ingredients carefully rebalanced to create something a bit different. My objective in creating Clever Cook recipes is to make sure that needless fuss is minimised and I have done my best to achieve that here. Only two pans and a serving dish to wash up – or better still, get someone else to wash up after the beautiful feast you've created.

Chicken and bacon pie

- Easy and different
- 45 minutes
Serves: 4

For the Potato Topping
3 large potatoes, peeled and
   cut into chunks
50g/2oz butter
1 tbsp Dijon mustard
100ml/3½fl oz milk

For the Filling
2 tbsp oil
½ onion, sliced
2 leeks, thinly sliced
115g/4oz streaky bacon,
   chopped up
8 large mushrooms, sliced
350g/12oz cooked chicken,
   cut into chunks
150ml/¼ pint gravy or chicken
   stock
4 tsp cream
salt and freshly ground black
   pepper

1. Boil the potatoes in salted water for about 15 minutes, or until soft.

2. Meanwhile, heat the oil for the filling in a large frying pan and fry the onion and leeks for 10 minutes, until soft. Add the bacon and fry for 5 more minutes. Turn up the heat and add the mushrooms and cook for 10 more minutes. Turn on the grill.

3. Mash the potatoes and add the butter, mustard and milk, mixing well. Season well.

4. Add the chicken and gravy or chicken stock to the bacon mixture and bring to a simmer. Heat through for 3–5 minutes and add the cream. Season judiciously. Put into a large shallow dish and top with the mashed potato, forking it over to cover the chicken. Brown under a hot grill.

Tip: *At Christmas, this recipe is also excellent for turkey leftovers.*

*Potato panache:
a few seconds spent finishing a dish so it looks pretty is time extremely well spent*

For me, kedgeree is the perfect all-in-one supper dish, fun to make and hugely popular. This version is finished with a light omelette rather than the traditional hard-boiled eggs.

An omelette lattice gives a stylish finishing touch

Chicken kedgeree

- Easy
- 40 minutes in all

Serves: 4

- Can be prepared ahead or frozen up to end of step 3

200g/8oz ordinary long-grain rice (a good mugful)
2 tbsp oil
1 onion, thinly sliced
1–2 tbsp curry paste or powder, depending on how much curry flavour you like
225–350g/8–12oz chicken (or turkey) boned, skinned breast fillet, cut into thin strips as if for a stir-fry
100g/4oz frozen peas
100g/4oz frozen prawns
good handful of parsley, finely chopped (3 generous tbsp), to serve
salt and freshly ground black pepper

For the Omelette
3 eggs
knob of butter

1. Put a big pan of salted water on to boil and when boiling, add the rice and cook for the higher cooking time recommended on the packet (usually 15 minutes).
2. Meanwhile, in a non-stick frying pan, heat the oil, add the onions and fry for 7 minutes, until beginning to go golden. Add the curry paste or powder and cook for 5 minutes more. Add the chicken and cook, stirring all the time, for 5 minutes more. Finally add the frozen peas and frozen prawns and cook for a further 5 minutes, until heated through.
3. Drain the rice thoroughly and return to the pan. Add the contents of the frying pan (reserving the pan), mix together and keep warm.
4. Just before serving, whip the eggs with some seasoning and a splash of water in a mug. Heat the butter in the frying pan until foaming and make a thin omelette (3 minutes only). Remove from heat.
5. To serve, mix the parsley into the kedgeree, season generously and spoon into a hot, large, shallow dish. Using a spatula, cut the omelette (still in the pan) into about 8 long thin strips and lay across the kedgeree in a rough lattice. Grind some pepper over and serve.

Tip: *Some cooks say they can't cook rice. Use a big pan, masses of boiling water and time the cooking carefully. No need to rinse after draining.*

I found the basis of this recipe in a fascinating little book called *Appealing Potatoes*. The author doesn't explain where Cinderella comes into it, though as she was a genuine princess herself perhaps she was displaying solidarity. In any case, thank you Princess Weikersheim – she used to live a village away from me – for the inspiration.

Cinderella potatoes

- Very easy
- 1 hour baking, 20 minutes to finish
Serves: 2 as a supper dish

1 large baking potato (about 450g/1lb)
a little olive oil
15g/½oz butter
2 tbsp milk
cayenne pepper
100g/4oz prawns, chopped
2 eggs
25g/1oz cheddar cheese
sea salt and freshly ground black pepper

1. Preheat oven to 200°C/fan oven 180°C/gas 6. Prick the potato with a fork or skewer, rub with oil and salt (preferably sea salt). Bake for 1 hour until tender.
2. Allow to cool slightly. Halve potato and scoop out the flesh, leaving enough so that the potato holds its shape. Mash with the butter and milk, then season with salt, pepper and cayenne and lightly mix in the chopped prawns.
3. Pile back into the potato shells and make an indentation in the top. Break an egg into this and grate over the cheese. Put back into the oven for 15 minutes, until the eggs are lightly set and the cheese melted but not browned.

Tip: *Defrost prawns quickly by soaking in hot water for 5 minutes and draining.*

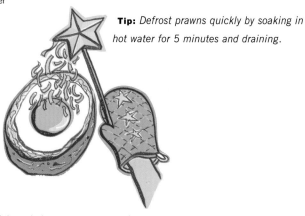

The potato flesh is mashed with prawns, returned to its shell and baked with an egg and cheese on top

This version of fish pie is distinctly upbeat, and dedicated to all those who thought they didn't like it.

As with all fish pies, there's quite a bit of washing up – but I've spared you the trouble of making a white sauce.

Mushrooms and a light touch put a smile on the face of old-fashioned fish pie

Fish and mushroom pie

- Not difficult
- 40 minutes preparation
- 25 minutes cooking

Serves: 4

- If made with fresh ingredients can be frozen; freeze at end of step 3
- Reheats well

750g/1lb 10oz potatoes
450g/1lb cod or haddock fillets
300ml/½ pint milk
2 eggs
115g/4oz mushrooms
40g/1½oz butter
handful of parsley
295g tin of Campbell's condensed mushroom soup
salt and freshly ground black pepper

1. If planning to cook at once, preheat oven to 180°C/fan oven 160°C/gas 4. Peel the potatoes, cut into chunks and boil in salted water until cooked, about 15 minutes. Meanwhile, poach the fish in a wide pan in the milk, lightly salted, for 8–10 minutes. Boil the eggs gently for 10 minutes until hard-boiled. Wipe and slice the mushrooms and fry in half the butter on a strong heat until brown, about 10 minutes. Chop the parsley.

2. Drain the potatoes, lift out fish (saving the milk, which should be about 250ml/9fl oz) and put the eggs in cold water to cool. Mash the potatoes and add 170ml/6fl oz of the reserved milk and the rest of the butter.

3. Assembly time. Use a shallow 1.2 litre/2-pint ovenproof dish. Discard any skin from the fish and put into the dish in bite-size pieces. Shell the eggs and slice into the dish. Mix the mushrooms in gently. Add 1 tbsp of the parsley and half the soup. Top with the potato mixture and fork over attractively.

4. Bake for 25 minutes, until very hot and beginning to bubble at the edges. While the pie is heating, put the remainder of the soup in a pan with 85ml/3fl oz of the milk (should be the exact amount you have left) and the rest of the parsley to make a sauce. Serve with frozen peas.

Tip: *Always fry mushrooms over a strong, constant heat to keep them sealed, or the juices run and you end up stewing them.*

Gina's Brazilian fish pie

- Can't go wrong
- 1 hour active work
- 15–20 minutes to bake

Serves: 2–3

- Can be prepared ahead up to end of step 5 but not frozen

450g/1lb potatoes
2 eggs (or 3 if serving 3)
350g/12oz smoked haddock
    fillet
milk
2 onions
25g/1oz butter
about 30 pitted black olives
    (half a 350g/12oz tin,
    drained)
4 tbsp extra virgin olive oil
salt and freshly ground black
    pepper

This is an adaptation by my friend Gina Marreco of a Portuguese dish using salt cod – *bacalhau à gomes de sá*. Gina, who has come to live in a village near me and has added her *Carioca* sparkle to the local social scene, discovered it worked just as well using smoked haddock, and the dish raises oohs and aahs at lunch parties. It is also very good with a tomato salad.

This is enough to serve 2 generously or 3, but the dish can easily be scaled up or down. Making it is a bit like being the conductor of an orchestra, bringing in the different instruments until the *tutti* at step 5. I will admit that, like all fish pies, it uses every pot and pan in the kitchen, but it can be made well in advance and reheated to make up for this inconvenience.

1. Preheat oven to 190°C/fan oven 170°C/gas 5. Peel potatoes, cut roughly and boil till soft in salted water. Fish them out into a colander and put the eggs into the same water; boil them for 8 minutes to lightly hardboil them and put them in cold water to cool.
2. Meanwhile, put the haddock in a pan, just cover with a mixture of half milk, half water seasoned with ground pepper. Bring to a simmer. Cook for 4 minutes and drain. Skin if necessary.
3. Meanwhile (by now you're doing at least three things at once, and it's by no means over yet) skin and slice the onions as thinly as you can. Heat the butter in a large frying pan and fry the onions slowly for 8–10 minutes, over a moderate heat, until soft and tinged with gold but do not brown them.
4. And while this is going on, roughly cut up the olives and get out a 1.2 litre/2-pint deep baking dish.

5. Assembly time at last. Crush the potato with a fork so it retains some texture. Flake half the fish into the bottom of the dish and top with half the onion and half the potato. Repeat with the remaining fish, onion and potato. Roughly cut the shelled eggs on top of this, season, then sprinkle over the olives and drizzle the olive oil over that.

6. Heat through for just 15–20 minutes in the oven.

Tip 1: *Smoked haddock comes in Toys"Я"Us yellow or a more natural smokey gold. It goes without saying that the former is packed with food colouring – probably the sort that makes you hyperactive. If you need perking up maybe it's a good idea; the two types taste pretty much the same to me.*

Tip 2: *When extra virgin olive oil first hit the news I used it for everything – with patchy results. Now I save it strictly for when I want a strong olivey taste and for flavouring pasta, risottos and other Mediterranean dishes.*

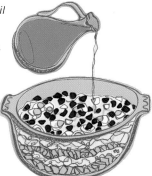

Layer up the ingredients

This brilliantly simple pasta dish is from one of my favourite Italian cooks, Susanna Gelmetti. It is fresh and vibrant, and the only real skill involved is tracking down some decent tomatoes which can be rather difficult. But I have found that if you buy carefully, and ripen on the windowsill at home, you can satisfy that yen for something summery without it being too much of a betrayal.

Lemon, tomato and ricotta pasta

- Easy
- No cooking except the pasta
- 5 minutes to prepare
- 10 minutes to cook

Serves: 4

250g/9oz dried pasta shapes – quills or twists
250g/9oz cherry tomatoes
zest of a lemon
250g/9oz tub of ricotta
2 tbsp extra virgin olive oil
good handful of fresh herbs
freshly grated parmesan
salt and freshly ground black pepper

1. Put a large pan of salted water on to boil and boil the pasta for the time recommended on the packet but do check to see it is done as I find the times on the packets are sometimes on the short side.

2. Meanwhile, halve the cherry tomatoes. Grate the lemon zest. Mix the ricotta in a bowl, add the lemon, salt and plenty of pepper and then fold in the tomatoes lightly with the oil.

3. When the pasta is cooked, drain and add to the ricotta mixture. Stir round well and return to the pan to heat through briefly. Add the herbs, chopped or torn up roughly, and a little parmesan and mix in. Check seasoning – it needs plenty.

4. Serve in bowls, scattered with extra parmesan.

Tip: *If I am grating lemons I look out for the unwaxed ones, which usually come in a set of four in plastic wrapping. They have a finer flavour, seem fresher and the scent of the zest is brighter and zingier. The drawback is that they don't keep as well as the waxed, although refrigerating them helps considerably. I am told that you can get the wax off regular lemons by washing in hot water, but I do not know how to tell if you have got it all off.*

A no-cook pasta sauce for supper

It is possible to make this tasty supper dish in 15 minutes. So without futher ado...

A dish that's economical of time, effort (and money)

1. Slice the bacon and throw into a frying pan. Sizzle for 6 minutes, till golden; if liquid comes out of the bacon, turn up the heat to evaporate it.

2. Meanwhile, put on a large pan of salted water, and when it comes to the boil add the penne. My packet says 12 minutes (fresh is usually 5 minutes).

3. While this is all going on, wash and trim the leeks and slice as finely as you can. Remove the bacon from the pan to a piece of kitchen paper, squeezing the pieces to leave the fat in the pan. Heat the pan once more and fry the leeks for 6 minutes, till brown.

4. Meanwhile, grate the cheddar and put to one side. When the pasta is ready, drain. When the leeks are ready, return the bacon to the pan with them. Put the pasta back in its pan with the mascarpone, stir round and add the bacon and leek to reheat.

5. Serve at once, with grated cheese and a drizzle of oil, if desired.

Tip: *The best speed-up tip I know is to multi-task – in other words, do as many things at once as you can. I also believe this is good practice for the brain, though I have no concrete evidence for this.*

Penne with bacon, leek and mascarpone

Suppers and main courses

- Dead easy
- 15 minutes if you do exactly as I say, in the order I suggest

Serves: 2

- Eat immediately

4 thickish rashers of rindless smoked bacon (about 140g/5oz)
225g/8oz dried penne (or fresh is even quicker)
2 leeks
85g/3oz cheddar cheese
115g/4oz mascarpone
2 tbsp extra virgin olive oil, optional

Martina's monkfish with lentils

• Easy; but not to be hurried
• 10 minutes to prepare
• 45 minutes to cook
Serves: 4

1 onion
1 tbsp olive oil
1 clove of garlic
250g/9oz green lentils
1.4 litres/2½ pints vegetable or
    other stock
6 bay leaves (see tip)
1 tsp balsamic or other vinegar
a little mustard
2 tbsp olive oil or extra virgin
    olive oil
salt and freshly ground black
    pepper

For the Monkfish
200–250g/8–9oz smoked back
    bacon (6–8 slices)
450g/1lb monkfish, filleted
cocktail sticks
2 tbsp olive oil
fresh coriander

This is something of a designer dish, combining several fashionable ingredients – lentils, balsamic vinegar, monkfish – and it was created by one of my most stylish friends, Martina Langer. Martina's natural habitat is the exclusive London restaurant, but if you could see her salsa-ing round her kitchen in her Gucci apron you would know that she is a natural cook, both inventive and practical.

1. Chop the onion and heat the oil in a large casserole. Fry for 4 minutes until softening, and add the garlic, crushed, for a further minute. Rinse the lentils and add to the saucepan with the stock and bay leaves. Bring to the boil and boil rapidly, half covered with a lid, for 10 minutes. Reduce heat to a simmer and cook fully covered for 35 minutes longer. There should be very little liquid left (if the lentils look dry while simmering, add extra boiling water). Drain the lentils, discard the bay leaves and dress with the vinegar, mustard and oil, whisked together with salt and pepper. Keep warm in a wide serving dish – or make in advance and reheat.

2. De-rind the bacon and slice each rasher down the centre to make two long thin strips. Count them. Cut the monkfish into the same number of cubes (fold the thinner pieces double to make good squat shapes). Coil a piece of bacon round each fish cube and spear diagonally with a cocktail stick (for neatness, try and spear the two bacon ends as you do so).

3. Heat the oil with the bacon rind and sizzle for 5 minutes to draw the fat from the rind; discard rind. (If in a hurry just throw away the rind and heat the oil). Fry the monkfish cubes, turning frequently, for 5 minutes until stiffened but tender when prodded with a knife. Season with black pepper, lay on to the hot lentils and strew with chopped coriander.

Tip 1: *Yes, it does seem a lot of bay leaves. Martina explains that they are intended to flavour the lentils, not just provide a background note, which is what you usually use them for.*

Tip 2: *Trendy cooks whose storecupboard is brimming with extra virgin this and balsamic that can use them here, but the dish will taste excellent using the plainer options.*

Coil the bacon round the monkfish cubes and spear neatly

This moreish recipe originates from my mother, who first cooked it in 1973 when I was a mere 15 and hardly knew potatoes needed peeling. It is a bit like a potato pizza.

Potato galette

Suppers and main courses

- Easy
- 25 minutes preparation
- 30 minutes in the oven

Serves: 4 as a supper dish

- Best eaten at once

680g/1½lb potatoes (4–5 medium-sized)
1 medium onion
175g/6oz cheddar cheese
6 small tomatoes
225g/8oz smoked streaky bacon
50g/2oz butter
2 tbsp milk
1 egg
salt and ground black pepper (see tip)

1. Preheat the oven to 200°C/fan oven 180°C/gas 6. Peel the potatoes, cut up and boil in salted water for about 15 minutes, or until soft.

2. Meanwhile, grate the onion (on the coarse side of the grater) and the cheese. Halve the tomatoes and chop the bacon roughly. Line a baking sheet with a piece of baking paper or greased greaseproof. Drain the potatoes and mash well with the butter, milk and egg. Beat in the onion, two thirds of the cheese, salt and plenty of finely ground pepper.

3. Pile on to the baking paper and form into a 23cm/9-inch disc, a bit like a pizza base. Arrange the tomatoes and bacon on top and flick over the rest of the cheese.

4. Bake for 25–30 minutes until nicely browned. Using a palette knife or spatula slide onto a large serving plate and cut into wedges. You could serve with sausages or eggs, but this is really a supper dish in itself.

Tip: *A piece of wisdom from TV superchef Gary Rhodes: coarsely ground pepper is excellent in most circumstances, but in mashed potato, the sort bought finely ground is much better, with a better flavour and no surprise crunching on bits of peppercorn.*

It looks a bit like a pizza, but instead of bread the base is crisp and tasty potato cake

Everyone loves macaroni cheese, despite the fact it almost always disappoints. The tinned version is slimy, and most recipes involve long-winded white sauces that are a hassle to make and rather tasteless when you get down to them. For this version I don't make a sauce at all – I simply mix ingredients. Very good with a tomato salad of good ripe tomatoes tossed in olive oil, salt, pepper and a pinch of sugar.

1. Bring a large pan of salted water to the boil. When it boils, put the macaroni on to cook for the longer recommended time on the packet.

2. While waiting for the water, get out your grater. Grate the cheddar on to a plate. Grate the parmesan on to another plate. Snip the spring onion tops on to the cheddar. Finally, grate the zest of the lemon on to the cheddar. Preheat the grill to high.

3. When the macaroni is cooked, drain in a colander. Don't wash up the pan, but put in the mascarpone, cheddar, mustard, spring onion tops and lemon zest. When melted, add the pasta and mix. Finally, fold in the gorgonzola cubes. Season with pepper – probably no salt needed – and turn into a shallow wide dish.

4. Shower with the parmesan, then add 6 or 7 flecks of butter. Grill for 5 minutes or until browned, watching carefully. Grind over some pepper and serve.

Tip: *Macaroni comes in many sizes. If you have a choice, the bigger the better.*

Most dishes are improved by a touch of onion flavouring. This is supplied instantly by spring onion tops, chopped with scissors

Real macaroni cheese

● Surprisingly easy (no white sauce to make)
● 35 minutes cooking and preparation
Serves: 4–6
● Can be reheated on a gentle heat, stirring (but do not boil)

250g/9oz dried macaroni
100g/4oz cheddar
50g/2oz parmesan
3 tbsp snipped spring onion stalks or chives
zest of a lemon
250g/9oz mascarpone
2 tsp Dijon mustard
115g/4oz gorgonzola cheese, cut into 1cm/½-inch cubes
a little butter
freshly ground black pepper

This is a great American supper dish – a really tasty combination of ingredients. Beetroot is an incredibly fashionable ingredient these days, and I am glad to say you can now buy cooked, vacuum-packed beets all year round. The vinegary kind is not suitable for this recipe.

Red flannel hash

- Easy and really tasty
- 15 minutes to put together
- 25 minutes to cook
Serves: 2

1 large potato, scrubbed but
    not peeled
knob of butter
1 small onion
2 tbsp olive oil
1 clove of garlic, crushed
2 small cooked beetroots,
    roughly chopped
200g/8oz corned beef
205g can of baked beans,
    drained
good shake of Worcestershire
    sauce
2 large eggs, optional
salt and freshly ground black
    pepper

1. Quarter the potato and put on to boil in salted water. When tender, drain, peel off the skin, which will come away instantly, and put in a bowl. Crush (don't mash) with a fork and add the butter.

2. Preheat the grill. Thinly slice the onion and fry in half the olive oil for 5 minutes until just becoming golden. Add the crushed garlic and cook for 1 minute, then add the beetroot. When all is hot and amalgamated, add to the potato and mix – it should be soft but not at all sloppy. Finally fold in the corned beef, cubed, and the drained baked beans. Add the Worcestershire sauce and taste for seasoning.

3. Heat the remaining olive oil in a non-stick frying pan, pile in the mixture and fry for 5 minutes. Now grill the top surface for 5 minutes longer. Either serve at once or if including eggs, make two deep indentations on top, break in the eggs and grill for about 3 minutes, till set.

Tip: *You do need to drain the baked beans as the liquid will make the mixture sloppy and stop it browning deliciously.*

A tasty Technicolor supper for 2

This romantically named casserole was served to me by a friend who entertains masterfully in a little flat near Victoria station – David Destiny.

1. Preheat oven to 150°C/fan oven 130°C/gas 2. Quarter the beets. Trim the steak and cut into regular 5cm/2-inch cubes and leave to dry on kitchen paper.

2. In a large flameproof casserole with a lid, heat half the oil and add the onions. Fry, covered, for 5–7 minutes.

3. Meanwhile, put the flour, ginger, seasoning and meat into a plastic carrier bag and shake up until the meat is well dusted.

4. In a large non-stick frying pan, heat the rest of the oil and fry the meat in two batches, turning frequently, for 5 minutes; it should be sealed and the blood just starting to run. Add to the onions in the casserole.

5. Meanwhile, put the garlic into a liquidiser or food processor and whizz until obliterated. Add beets, orange zest and juice, sugar or syrup and stock and whizz again till smooth.

6. Pour over the meat mixture, add bay leaves and cover the casserole with the lid. Cook in the oven for 1¾ hours, stirring two or three times. Remove the lid and cook for another half hour. Stir in cream just before serving and sprinkle parsley on top.

Tip: *I find this is the perfect temperature for stewing chuck steak, though it needs at least 2 and preferably 3 hours to turn to melting tenderness.*

Sumptuous in flavour, brilliant in colour

Red velvet goulash

- Not difficult
- 30 minutes to prepare
- 2¼ hours in oven
Serves: 4
- Can be reheated or frozen

500g/1lb 2oz (two of the usual 250g/9oz plastic wrapped packs) pre-cooked beetroot (choose ones that look fresh and brightly coloured)
900g/2lb chuck steak – preferably not pre-diced
2 tbsp oil
1 large or 2 medium onions, sliced
2 tbsp flour
2 tsp ground ginger
3 cloves of garlic, peeled and quartered
zest and juice of 2 oranges
1 tbsp of sugar, or syrup from a jar of stem ginger
200ml/7fl oz beef stock
2 bay leaves
salt and freshly ground black pepper

To finish
142ml carton of soured cream or crème fraîche
generous handful of parsley

Roast chicken with yogurt, honey and lemon

Suppers and main courses

- A delicious change
- Start the night before
- 15 minutes to prepare
- 1–1¼ hours to cook
- Allow an extra 15 minutes to prepare the stuffing

Serves: 4

1.6kg/3½lb free-range chicken

For the Marinade
150ml/¼ pint plain yogurt
1 tbsp runny honey
1 lemon
2 tsp ground sumach, optional (see tip)
salt and freshly ground black pepper

For the Olive Stuffing, optional
100g/4oz bacon
1 small onion
100g/4oz small black olives, stoned and chopped
1 tsp dried thyme

Roast chicken is such a good thing that I am always looking for ways to give it a spin. This has a vaguely Middle Eastern feel to it, and you can emphasise this if you can find a very unusual spice – sumach. This is by no means necessary to the finished effect, but it makes the dish look pretty and adds depth to the lemon flavour. My colleague at *Good Food*, Sarah Jane Evans, whose wisdom in unexpected areas frequently amazes me, tells me that sumach is used instead of lemon in certain Middle Eastern dishes, having a gently sour taste.

I am also proposing a stuffing. This is very good – and works extremely well for guinea fowl, if there are only two of you and you fancy a slightly extravagant change from chicken.

1. The night before, mix together the yogurt, honey, lemon zest and juice but save the squeezed lemons to stuff the chicken if you aren't making the stuffing (see step 2). If using the sumach, add half. Season well and rub all over the washed and dried chicken (but not the cavity), including, if you wish, under the skin of the chicken. Though it requires a bit of care, putting flavourings under the skin of a chicken is the best way of getting a really tasty result. To do it, take off any rings that might tear the skin and, with the chicken legs away from you, wiggle your fingers under the flap of skin at the back and up each side, gently separating the breast from the skin. Then work in some of the yogurt mixture. Leave the chicken covered overnight in the fridge, and bring to room temperature before cooking.

2. Put a roasting tin and rack in the oven and preheat the oven to 190°C/fan oven 170°C/gas 5. If you want to stuff the chicken, chop the bacon and onion finely (the work of seconds in a food processor) and fry

without oil for 6–7 minutes. Take off the heat and mix in the olives and the thyme. Add pepper but no extra salt. Spoon into the cavity of the chicken. If you are not stuffing the chicken, put the squeezed lemon halves and the onion, skinned and sliced, into the cavity.

3. Lay the chicken on one breast on the preheated roasting rack. Spoon over all the marinade left in the dish. Roast for 20 minutes, then turn to the other breast and roast for 20 more minutes. Set the chicken the right way up, sprinkle with remaining sumach if using and finish roasting for a further 20 minutes, by which time the chicken will be a gorgeous mahogany colour. Check it is cooked.

4. Rest the bird for 20 minutes before serving, and let everyone spoon out the stuffing for themselves. Make gravy in the usual way with the pan juices, adding a final squeeze of lemon if you wish – particularly delicious.

Tip: *Sumach is a Persian spice, bright red in colour and with a sour taste. It is widely used in Arabia as a meat tenderiser, but is hard to find in Britain. If you know of a Lebanese or Iranian shop they usually stock it, but it is not available by mail order.*

Always start a roast chicken wrong side up – the juices flow towards the breast rather than straight into the tin

This is a traditional Italian way to cook a choice leg of spring lamb; the meat is soft and succulent, tender enough to cut with a fork, and the juices make a fragrant gravy.

Roman lamb

Suppers and main courses

- Straightforward
- 2½ hours to cook

Serves: 6

25g/1oz butter
3 tbsp olive oil
1.6kg/3½lb leg of spring lamb
3 cloves of garlic
2 sprigs of rosemary
150ml/¼ pint dry white wine
salt and freshly ground black
    pepper

For the Gravy
a knob of butter
1 tbsp flour

1. Preheat oven to 160°C/fan oven 150°C/gas 3. Select a large deep casserole with a lid. Melt the butter and oil in it, and when hot, add the lamb, garlic and rosemary. After 2 minutes, turn it over, and continue doing so every minute until browned on all sides (most legs of lamb have 6 surfaces to brown – you may need to hold the leg in position to ensure good browning of the last couple). Turn upside down (with the meatier side facing down), pour in the wine and season well. Bring to the boil, spoon over some of the juices, cover and put in the oven.

2. After half an hour, turn over, baste and season lightly. Put the lid back on and return to the oven, basting every ½ hour. After 2½ hours in total the lamb will melt in the mouth. Remove to a carving dish and make the gravy.

3. Either remove the juices with a bulb baster, leaving the fat behind, or pour all into a bowl and skim off the fat. Put the de-greased meat juices in a small pan and bring to a boil. Mash a knob of butter with 1 tbsp flour on a saucer till thoroughly combined, then whisk flakes of it into the boiling liquid (a gravy whisk is ideal). It will thicken slightly and add sheen. Check seasoning, carve the meat and serve.

Tip: *This sauce-thickening technique is known as a "beurre manié" and is a very useful emergency trick for thin or dull sauces.*

The correct way to carve a leg of lamb is to take a vertical V-shaped slice from the top, then continue taking wedge-shaped slices in each direction

This is an idea from the cook who many regard as the father of modern home cooking, Robert Carrier. His generous personality and lavish use of ingredients endeared him to cooks who had suffered too long from post-war shortages, and showed what could be done if only you let your hair down.

Purists may wonder what I am doing adding self-raising flour to pastry – but it does lift and lighten it, which works well here.

1. Make the pastry in a processor by whizzing together the flours, butter and some seasoning, then adding 2 tbsp cold water and up to an extra teaspoon more, until the mixture just combines. If convenient, shape into a ball and refrigerate for 20 minutes, otherwise use immediately. Preheat oven to 190°C/fan oven 170°C/gas 5. Line a deep 23–25cm/9–10-inch tin and bake blind for 15 minutes. Remove baking beans and foil and finish for 5 minutes uncovered.
2. Meanwhile make the filling. Either in a mixer or by hand, cream the cream cheese with the blue cheese and butter. Beat in the eggs, cream or milk, and herbs. When it is fairly smooth, pour into the tart shell and bake for 25–30 minutes until pleasantly golden.

Tip: *You will notice that I don't insist you chill the pastry before baking blind. We are told that chilling prevents shrinkage, but pastry always shrinks a little, and in this recipe at least it presents no problem.*

A light but piquant savoury first course or lunch dish

Roquefort quiche

- Easy
- 30 minutes to prepare
- 45 minutes to cook

Serves: 8

- Freezes well

100g/4oz plain flour
50g/2oz self-raising flour
85g/3oz butter
salt and freshly ground black pepper

For the Filling
200g/8oz pack of Philadelphia cream cheese
100g/4oz pack of Roquefort
1 tbsp butter, softened
3 eggs
300ml/½ pint cream or milk
good handful of chives and parsley, finely chopped

A very easy dish, especially if you have a flameproof gratin dish that you can use on the stove and then transfer to the oven. Excellent with green beans or mange-tout.

Salmon fillets with a sesame crust

- Very easy
- 5 minutes to prepare
- 12 minutes to cook

Serves: 2

2 slices of salmon fillet, skin on
1 tbsp sesame seeds
25g/1oz butter
2 tsp sesame oil
1 tbsp dry sherry
salt and freshly ground
    black pepper

1. Preheat the oven to 180°C/gas 4. Put the salmon on a board, skin side up, season and pat on the sesame seeds. Heat the butter and half the sesame oil in a small iron gratin dish on the stove.

2. When sizzling, add the salmon, skin side down, and fry for 5 minutes. Check the sesame seeds are lightly brown but do not turn. Sprinkle the sherry over the upper side, spoon over the buttery juices and the rest of the sesame oil, season well and put in the oven for 6–7 minutes, until cooked but still tender.

Tip: *Some people don't like the skin of fish, but if you do something with it, as in this recipe, it's an extra treat*

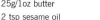

Open sesame – a nutty idea for the elegant salmon fillet

This is a simple supper based on the ubiquitous salmon steak. Once a luxury, this pretty coloured fish has now become so popular you can get a little bit bored with it. The recipe is based on an idea by the inventive cook Lindsey Bareham, who taught me that if you cook leeks with butter and some liquid, they can be liquidised into a creamy sauce that you would swear is packed with cream and calories, but is actually as light as air.

1. Preheat the oven to 180°C/gas 4. Sprinkle the salmon steaks with some of the lemon juice and seasoning, cover with foil and then bake for 20–25 minutes. Check the steaks are cooked.

2. Meanwhile, wash the leeks well, quarter lengthwise and then slice into 1cm/½-inch pieces. Cook in the butter, covered, for 10 minutes, by which time they should be tender. Add the sherry or Martini and cook for 7 minutes, till the liquid has mainly boiled away. Then add the fish stock or vegetable water and cook quickly for 3 minutes longer. Liquidise and return to pan, then season. Add cream and some more lemon juice to taste. Set aside.

3. Squeeze a little more lemon juice on the salmon and serve on the leek cream, into which you have stirred some finely shredded spinach, lettuce or sorrel.

Tip: *Finely shredded, lettuce can always be used as a garnish. It adds a pleasant crunch and a slight pepperiness.*

Cook the leeks gently and they melt into a creamy sauce

Salmon steaks with leek cream

- Easy
- 5 minutes to prepare
- 30 minutes to cook
- **Serves: 4**

4 salmon steaks
juice of a lemon
4 leeks
50g/2oz butter
200ml/7fl oz dry sherry or Martini
200ml/7fl oz fish stock, or water from cooking vegetables
4 tbsp crème fraîche
a little spinach, lettuce or sorrel
salt and freshly ground black pepper

This was the first recipe ever to appear in the Clever Cook column, and was created as a sort of manifesto: food that is quick, satisfying and capable of being adapted to suit your personal taste, or what you happen to have in the fridge. Serve it with a crisp green salad.

Sausage, tomato and herb pasta

• Easy
• 35 minutes to cook
Serves: 4
• Can be frozen and gently reheated

1 tbsp oil
450g/1lb sausages
3 spring onions, cut up small
250g/9oz tomatoes
200g/8oz dried pasta shapes – penne are excellent
¾ tsp dried or a good handful of fresh sage (about 25 leaves), chopped finely
80g pack of Boursin pepper cream cheese
lots of grated parmesan, to serve

1. Put salted water on to boil for the pasta. Meanwhile, put the oil and sausages in a big frying pan and fry in the usual way. After 10 minutes, turn down the heat, add the onions and finish cooking (2–5 minutes more).
2. Unless you don't mind flecks of tomato skin in the finished dish, scald the tomatoes in boiling water for 10 seconds, then skin and slice them.
3. About 20 minutes before serving, boil the pasta as instructed on the packet – anything from 7–13 minutes.
4. Drain any oil from the frying pan and slice each sausage into 6, returning to the pan with the tomatoes and dried sage if using. If using fresh sage, don't put it in yet. Cook for 5–6 minutes to soften the tomatoes then, off the heat, mash in the Boursin and fresh sage, if using. Warm through gently while draining the pasta.
5. Mix in the pasta and serve with the grated parmesan cheese on top.

Tip: *If you can only find little tubs of dried parmesan, it's better to use grated cheddar – and don't stint.*

How you slice even the simplest ingredients can add real flair to a simple dish

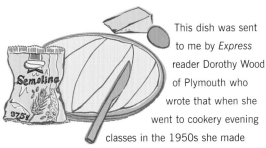

This dish was sent to me by *Express* reader Dorothy Wood of Plymouth who wrote that when she went to cookery evening classes in the 1950s she made this recipe from the Battersea Polytechnic Domestic Science Department's *Household Cookery* – price 2/6. The mixture is virtually identical to Italian gnocchi, and frying makes them extremely delicious.

1. Put the semolina and milk in a pan and bring to the boil, stirring all the time. Simmer for 6 minutes, till very thick – if you stop stirring it will stick. Off the heat, mix in the butter, cheese, nutmeg and plenty of seasoning. Hold a dinner plate under the tap to wet it thoroughly and pour off the water. Spoon the mixture on to the plate and smooth out. Leave to cool and set.

2. When cold, turn on to a board and cut into the shapes shown in the picture – resembling fish fillets. Dip in the beaten egg and then the breadcrumbs. Heat the oil, then fry the fillets in two batches for about 2–3 minutes per side.

3. If making the sauce, heat the cream with the garlic. Simmer gently for 5 minutes to reduce. Discard the garlic, stir in the parmesan, season with salt, pepper and Worcestershire sauce and heat gently. The sauce should be thick and rich. Serve with lemon slices and a dollop of sauce on each plate.

Tip: *This sauce recipe was a gift from a friend, Lady Dorothy Heber Percy. It is also excellent with ham and any time you want a quick rich white sauce.*

Semolina fillets

- Worth the trouble
- 20 minutes to prepare (allow time to cool)
- 20 minutes to cook

Serves: 3–4

50g/2oz semolina
300ml/½ pint milk
25g/1oz butter
40g/1½oz grated cheese
pinch of nutmeg
1 small egg, beaten
3 slices of bread, (crusts removed), made into breadcrumbs
2–3 tbsp sunflower oil, for frying
slices of lemon, to serve
salt and freshly ground black pepper

For the Quick Parmesan Sauce, optional
4 tbsp double cream
1 clove of garlic, peeled and sliced in half
2 tbsp grated parmesan
Worcestershire sauce

As ever, with this recipe the better the ingredients, the better the finished dish. I have recently discovered salted anchovies, rather than the ones in oil, and despite the fact you have to rinse them and fillet them, the flavour is much better. You can find them in good Italian delicatessens.

Sicilian spaghetti

- Quite a lot of ingredients, but dead easy to make
- 5 minutes to prepare
- 20 minutes to cook

Serves: 3–4

pinch of saffron
1 small onion
1 small bulb of fennel
1 tbsp olive oil
3 tbsp pine kernels
1 garlic clove
400g/14oz tin of tomatoes, undrained
3 tbsp sultanas or raisins
6 salted anchovies, rinsed, filleted and slivered, or a 50g/2oz tin, drained and slivered
splash of soda water or fizzy mineral water
350g/12oz best-quality dried spaghetti
toasted breadcrumbs or freshly grated parmesan, to serve (see tip)
salt and freshly ground black pepper

A jubilant dish from sunny Sicily

1. Bring a large pan of salted water to the boil for the spaghetti. Grind the saffron and pour over 1 tbsp boiling water; leave to soak. Slice the onion and fennel very finely, heat the oil and then fry them over a moderate heat for about 8 minutes, till the onion is golden, the fennel softened. Stir in the pine kernels and garlic and sizzle for 2 minutes longer. Add the tomatoes and their juice and the sultanas or raisins and season (easy on the salt). Simmer for 3–4 minutes until amalgamated, draw off the heat and add the anchovies. Set to one side.

2. Meanwhile, cook the spaghetti. As the spaghetti nears completion, warm the sauce and splash in a little fizzy water if it looks dry (the Italians say that fizzy water amalgamates the sauce better than ordinary, and I find this to be the case). Stir in the spaghetti and heat slowly for a good 3–4 minutes (another Italian trick which means the spaghetti really takes on the flavour of the sauce).

3. Serve either with toasted breadcrumbs or parmesan.

Tip: *Sicily has never been a wealthy island, and toasted breadcrumbs were their version of parmesan. I toast them with a little butter or oil in the oven – at 180°C/fan oven 160°C/gas 4 they take about 10 minutes to go golden, tossing occasionally.*

Belly of pork is something you may need to get your butcher to look into; ask him to take the bones out and score the top either in parallel lines or in a diamond pattern.

This dish is inspired by a Gary Rhodes recipe. Although it takes forever in the oven, you have virtually nothing to do, and you end up with a meltingly delicious roast and fab crackling.

1. Preheat the oven to 180°C/gas 4. Slice all the vegetables finely. Find a baking tin into which the pork will just fit when laid flat (this is important; too big a tin and the vegetable braise will dry out). Pile in the vegetables and season lightly. Lay the pork on top, rub with oil and sprinkle generously with sea salt.

2. Roast for 1½ hours, then reduce heat to 160°C/fan oven 140°C/gas 3 and roast for 2½ hours more. Add more liquid if the onions start to get too brown. Every hour or so, lift the pork with a fork and move the vegetables round so they cook evenly. Do not baste the crackling.

3. Carve and serve with baked or mashed potato, with the vegetables in the rich juices. If the onions look very fatty, lift out with a slotted spoon and dry on kitchen paper.

Tip: *Having made this many times, it is true to say that every piece of pork varies in liquid and fat content, and you simply have to watch it carefully while it's in the oven and add more water if the onions appear to dry out. There is nothing you can do to predict this, but the result will be absolutely melt-in-the-mouth either way.*

So tender, so good – melt-in-the-mouth slow cooked pork

Slow roast belly of pork

- Very easy
- 4 hours (yes, 4 hours) in the oven
Serves: 6–8

2 large onions
1 bulb fennel (or other robust vegetables)
2 sticks of celery
9 cloves
1.3–1.8kg/3–4lb belly of pork, boned
a little oil
sea salt and freshly ground black pepper

Stuffed cabbage

- Fun to make
- 30 minutes to prepare,
- 3 hours to bake

Serves: 6

- Can be prepared ahead

450g/1lb best quality
    sausagemeat
1 egg
1 fresh Savoy cabbage, not
    too big
600ml/1 pint gravy or stock, or
    mixture of stock and wine

This is a marvellous peasant dish from the provinces of France (where it might be termed *cuisine grand-mère*) and brought to this country by Jane Grigson. It is fun to make – do not be perturbed by the long cooking time, as the dish looks after itself entirely.

To raise it to the level of sublimity, braise the cabbage in some nice leftover gravy. Failing this use stock, wine or a mixture and then if you wish thicken it up to make a sauce at the last minute. The way I do this is to put a dessertspoon of soft butter on a plate with a dessertspoon of flour, mash them together with the back of a fork, and flick bits of the paste (which is called beurre manié) into the boiling liquid – whisking all the time. Boil for 2 minutes, whisking away, and you will have a gleaming sauce. Repeat if you want to thicken more.

1. Preheat the oven to 160°C/fan oven 140°C/gas 3. Put a large pan of salted water on to boil. Mix the sausagemeat and egg in a bowl. Get out string and scissors, and a large ovenproof pot, with a lid, that will hold the cabbage comfortably. Wash the cabbage and pull any coarse leaves off the outside, and cut the base so it stands straight. Carve out the centre of the stem from below, if you wish – the hard woody bit – but keep the cabbage fully intact.

2. Plunge the cabbage into the pan of water and boil for precisely 5 minutes. Remove and drain.

3. When cold enough to handle, slowly and patiently peel back all the leaves of the cabbage, like a flower. The outside leaves will still be hot, the centre scarcely warm. In the end you'll get to some tiny leaves in the centre. Stop.

4. Now scoop a scant tablespoon of sausagemeat mixture (not too much) and put it at the base of the last leaf you pulled back. Continue to do so, gradually

reassembling the cabbage and holding it in shape as you do. Keep the filling to the base of each leaf; it should not squeeze out.

5. Now tie the sausage in shape. Put a bit of string round the middle of the cabbage (the Equator, as it were) and tie. Then tie a couple of uprights, until it feels secure. If you were unlucky enough not to be born with three hands, here's a tip my butcher taught me: do an extra loop on the first stage of your knot and it will hold tight while you finish the knot. Not many people know that.

6. Put into the pot with the gravy or stock, cover with a butter paper or a little foil (to keep the top leaves moist) and a lid and bake for 3 hours, or until meltingly tender (the cabbage should be very soft indeed. The dish is accommodating and will continue baking happily for another hour if you wish. Slice as you would a cake, and serve with bread or, for complete rusticity, baked potatoes.

Tip: *Opening the cabbage out leaf by leaf you become aware of what an extraordinary work of art this humble vegetable is. Take your time and enjoy it.*

Open the cabbage out and put a little pocket of sausagemeat at the base of each leaf

Roasting duck in this way, with its rather unconventional baste, gives a marvellously moist and un-fatty texture, flavour and colour; your guests will never know how you have achieved it. The potatoes are based on a recipe by a Frenchman who is acclaimed as the greatest living chef (Joel Rebluchon); it looks odd on paper but it works.

Surprise roast duck with gratin dauphinoise

- Easy
- 20 minutes preparation
- 2 hours partially attended roasting

Serves: 4

- Any leftover potatoes are excellent reheated

For the duck
2kg/4½lb duck
1 can of Coca Cola (not Diet Coke)

For the potatoes
250ml/9fl oz milk
125ml/4fl oz double cream or crème fraîche
500g/1lb 2oz potatoes
50g/2oz cheddar cheese
a little nutmeg
25g/1oz butter
salt and freshly ground black pepper

1. Preheat oven to 200°C/fan oven 180°C/gas 6. Season the duck, put on a rack over a small roasting tin and place in the oven. After 20 minutes start basting with the Coca Cola, a few tablespoons at a time. Continue basting with about 6 tablespoons of Coca Cola (not the pan juices, which are too fatty) every 15 minutes until you have used it all. After 2 hours in total, check the duck is cooked and remove to a carving board. Make gravy with a little of the fat and stock, but discard the other juices, as a little Coca Cola goes a long way.

2. Meanwhile, prepare the gratin by putting the milk and cream in a medium pan and bringing to the boil. Peel and slice the potatoes as thinly as possible. Add most of the cheese to the cream mixture, then add the potatoes, season with salt, pepper and a little nutmeg and simmer gently, stirring often, until the potatoes are tender – 25–30 minutes (but do check). Season, transfer to a shallow ovenproof dish of 1 litre/1¾-pint capacity (not buttered), top with remaining cheese and butter and put in the oven on the shelf below the duck until golden – about 30 minutes.

See if your guests can divine the aromatic, almost oriental flavouring of the duck

Tip: *Prick the roast duck all over with a sharp skewer before and occasionally during cooking to make sure as much fat as possible is drained away.*

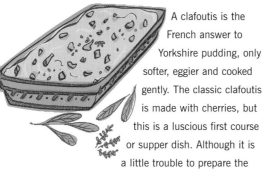

A clafoutis is the French answer to Yorkshire pudding, only softer, eggier and cooked gently. The classic clafoutis is made with cherries, but this is a luscious first course or supper dish. Although it is a little trouble to prepare the tomatoes, this really brings out their flavour, and makes even rather ordinary tomatoes taste brilliant.

1. Preheat oven to 190°C/fan oven 170°C/gas 5. Skin the tomatoes, halve horizontally (along the Equator, as it were) and using your thumb and two fingers, scoop out the seeds in their jelly (I do this under running water). Cut each half in half again, sprinkle with salt and leave to dry on double thickness of kitchen paper while you make the batter.

2. Mix the eggs, yolks, cream, half the cheese and half the thyme. Season lightly.

3. Generously butter a large shallow baking dish (about 1.4 litre/2½ pint capacity). Dry the tomatoes with a final piece of kitchen paper, cut out any hard cores. Then lay them in the dish, seasoning with pepper (no more salt necessary). Pour over the batter, sprinkle with the remaining cheese and thyme and bake for 30 minutes. Serve warm or at room temperature.

Tip: *Choose large, not-too-ripe tomatoes, on the grounds they are quicker to peel, and over-ripe ones tend to fall to bits when you skin and seed them.*

Tomatoes in a golden eggy batter

Tomato clafoutis

- Easy
- 20 minutes to prepare
- 30 minutes to cook
- **Serves: 6**
- Freezes well

1kg/2lb 4oz ripe tomatoes
2 eggs, plus 2 yolks
5 tbsp double cream or crème fraîche
50g/2oz freshly grated parmesan
2 tsp fresh thyme or sage leaves, chopped
salt and freshly ground black pepper

The combination of rice, trout and sauce is unusual and delectable. Peas are the perfect accompaniment.

Trout with wild rice and mushrooms

- Worth the effort
- 20 minutes to prepare
- 55 minutes to cook

Serves: 4

- Freezes well

175g/6oz wild rice (or Tilda's wild rice and basmati rice mixed)
1 onion, chopped
250g/9oz well-flavoured mushrooms, such as chestnut or portabello, sliced
2 tbsp oil
clove of garlic, finely chopped or crushed
450g/1lb trout or salmon fillets
3 tbsp double cream or crème fraîche
small handful of parsley

For the Sauce
280g/10oz well-flavoured tomatoes
100g/4oz butter
2 egg yolks
1 tbsp sherry

A sophisticated mix of flavours and colours

1. Skin and seed the tomatoes, sprinkle with salt and put on kitchen paper in a colander to drain. Cook the wild rice in lots of salted boiling water for 50 minutes. Heat the oil and fry the onion and mushrooms till nicely browned, adding the garlic after 5 minutes.

2. Cook the fish. If grilling, season, dot with butter and put on foil; if baking, season and dot with butter, then wrap loosely in foil. Trout fillets take 12–15 minutes at 190°C/fan oven 170°C/gas 5, or 7–8 minutes under the grill (turn the latter half way through). Remove any skin and break into large chunks – if there are any fishy juices, keep them too.

3. Fold the drained rice, onion mixture, fish and juices together gently and stir in the cream. Check seasoning, put in a dish and keep warm. Chop the parsley.

4. Just before serving, cut up the tomatoes and liquidise with the egg yolks in the bowl of a food processor which you have warmed with hot water (this ensures the sauce cooks as it whizzes). Heat the butter until boiling. Take the butter off the heat, add the sherry to cool it slightly, then with the food processor running, pour slowly through the funnel of machine on to the egg-tomato mixture: it will thicken as you do this. (If the mixture curdles, the butter was too hot. If it doesn't thicken, tomatoes or butter were not hot enough: return to the pan and stir gingerly over a gentle heat until it thickens.) Sprinkle parsley over the trout and serve with the sauce.

Tip: *Wild rice is cooked when the grains open up. If serving as an accompaniment, season well and add some butter while still hot.*

Vegetables

Step into any supermarket nowadays and it's as if you've entered the garden of Eden. Yet I would always rather cook with familiar vegetables, preferably ones that have been grown in this country and if possible during their natural season. Beautiful fresh vegetables, simply cooked, are hard to beat, but this chapter contains a few savoury suggestions for when you feel you like a change.

If you haven't discovered it yet, wild rice is a flavoursome alternative to ordinary rice (see also page 54). It isn't really rice at all – it's a long grain marsh grass (*Zizania aquatica*) and has been a staple food of the Sioux and Chippewa American Indians for centuries. The grains swell up during cooking into a clove-like shape. It tastes slightly spicy, looks pretty (black, fawn and grey) and is much less expensive than it used to be.

American stuffed mushrooms

● Easy
● 10 minutes to prepare
● 30 minutes to cook
Serves: 4–8 depending on size of mushrooms

100g/4oz wild rice
4 large field mushrooms
1 small onion or 3 spring onions
1 thick rasher of smoked bacon, or your favourite bacon
1 tbsp olive oil, plus a little extra
85g/3oz St Agur cheese, or other soft strong blue cheese
small bunch parsley or tarragon, finely chopped
25g/1oz freshly grated parmesan
salt and freshly ground black pepper

1. Put a large pan of salted water on to boil, and a kettle. Add the rice and cook for the time recommended on the packet, then drain, rinse with the boiling water and leave till ready.

2. Meanwhile, clean the mushrooms and remove the stems. Chop the stems, chop the onion and bacon and fry together in the oil for 8 minutes (you can add the bacon rind in one piece if you like, to add flavour, and discard after frying). Allow to cool for a couple of minutes (important as you don't want the cheese to melt too much at this point), then stir in the cheese, roughly chopped, rice, parsley or tarragon and freshly ground black pepper (it will not need salt).

3. About 15 minutes before eating, heat the grill. Brush the top (convex) side of the mushrooms with oil and season well, then grill for 5–8 minutes, till sizzling. Carefully turn over, brush the inside with oil. Spoon the filling on to the mushrooms neatly, top with the parmesan and brown – about 3 minutes more. You may have a little leftover filling – this can be frozen and used as an individual treat in the future.

Tip: *Tilda makes packs of mixed basmati and wild rice which are excellent and can be used in this recipe – follow packet directions. Or you can use regular rice.*

A fascinating and different rice to try out

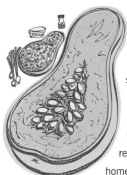

For several years I've admired those tempting pale orange butternut squashes you see in supermarkets, but I've never known what to do with them. Here is an idea from the United States, inspired by a recipe by America's favourite homemaker, Martha Stewart (if you haven't come across her, she's a sort of Betty Crocker-Delia Smith-Jane Asher rolled into one). For something as delectable, it's surprisingly low in fat, and makes a good simple supper, followed by fruit or cheese.

1. Preheat the oven to 200°C/gas 6. Halve the squash lengthwise and remove the seeds and coarse fibres. Season well and put in a roasting tin half full of water. Cover the whole thing with foil and bake for about 40 minutes until tender but not collapsing.
2. Remove from the oven, drain and cool on a board for a few moments. Scrape the flesh into a bowl, leaving a thin margin of flesh so the squash retains its shape. Mix the flesh with paprika, chopped chives, the crème fraîche and more seasoning. Pile back into the shells, top with breadcrumbs and finish in the oven for 15 minutes until lightly browned.

Tip: *Because the marrow family is so watery, I think veg that belong to it are always better served with something to add a bit of crunch. The first cookery competition I ever entered I won with an invention involving marrow and croutons – you need to drain the marrow very well after cooking and add garlicky croutons at the last second. Toasted almonds are another good idea.*

Brown the squash in the oven with a crunchy breadcrumb topping

Baked butternut squash

Vegetables

● Very easy
● About 1 hour (but very little work involved)
Serves: 2, (or 4 as an accompaniment)

1 butternut squash, weighing about 675g/1½lb
paprika
small handful chives or spring onion tops
3 tbsp low-fat crème fraîche
1 thick slice of bread, crust removed and crumbled into breadcrumbs
salt and freshly ground black pepper

A pair of recipes for two great salad vegetables – both of which can be cooked to great advantage, bringing out their slightly bitter crunch. Both are good with plain meat dishes.

Braised chicory in sherry and Little Gems fried in butter

Vegetables

- Easy
- 1 hour
Serves: 4

For the Chicory
4 bulbs of chicory
25g/1oz butter
4 tbsp dry sherry
150ml/¼ pint stock

For the Little Gems
4 Little Gem lettuces
clove of garlic
50g/2oz butter and a little oil

1. For the **chicory** preheat oven to 200°C/fan oven 180°C/gas 6. Halve the bulbs vertically. Trim out the tough core.

2. Heat the butter in a large ovenproof dish – cast iron is ideal. Add the chicories and sear over a high heat for 6–8 minutes, by which time they should be a good nutty brown all over. Do not rush this part, as this is what gives them their lovely caramelised flavour.

3. Pour over the sherry, which will evaporate almost at once, and season. Pour over the stock, bring to the boil and put in the oven.

4. Bake for a full 40 minutes, until the stock is almost evaporated, the chicory tender. Serve from the dish.

5. For the **Little Gems** trim the lettuce and quarter lengthwise. Trim the core, which can be a little bitter. Rub the lettuce all over with a cut side of garlic. Heat the butter and oil until the butter foams and then subsides – it needs to be good and hot. Add the lettuce and fry, turning all the time, until brown and slightly scorched all over – about 10 minutes in all – season and serve.

Tip: *Chicory goes brown after you cut it but obviously this is no problem in a dish where you want it to be golden, so do not worry about lemon juice and so on.*

Slice both the chicory and baby lettuces to make long thin elegant shapes

This is so good and tasty you could almost pass it off as a main course.

Some gourmets yearn for plum tomatoes from Tuscany or anchovies from southern Spain, but give me a good crisp British cabbage and I'm in heaven. I was talking to food expert Henrietta Green about this – it's such a pity we've forgotten about wonderful native British ingredients (to say nothing of the seasons). Part of the problem is that even if the cabbage was grown in the field next door to your house it has been to Aylesbury and back, and has inevitably lost its freshness and good humour on the journey.

1. Wash and quarter the cabbage and cook in boiling salted water for about 10 minutes until just cooked. Drain very thoroughly.
2. Heat the butter (use the pan you've just cooked the cabbage in if suitable) and fry the gammon or bacon, for 4 minutes until it is golden and starts to pop. Remove from the heat.
3. Turn the cabbage on to a board and shred finely. Add to the gammon or bacon with the sage leaves, if using, and cream cheese, and over a low heat stir round till all is hot and melted. Stir in the parmesan, heat again till it begins to melt and serve.

Tip: *I always prefer to boil cabbage in large pieces and shred it afterwards, as it keeps more of its crunch. If you are into steaming, you could also steam the cabbage.*

A rich mixture of cabbage, bacon and cream cheese

Cabbage with a twist

Vegetables

● Easy
● 25 minutes from start to finish
Serves: 4
● Good with cold meat and a jacket potato

1 cabbage – the hard green type are best
25g/1oz butter
85g/3oz smoked gammon steak, finely diced or smoked bacon, finely sliced
half a dozen sage leaves, optional, chopped
100g/4oz cream cheese, such as Philadelphia
25g/1oz freshly grated parmesan

This is flavoursome enough to be served as a first course, though it is really designed as an accompaniment. I especially like it with pork chops or roast pork, though it is good with any fairly plain meat dish; it is a bit of a fiddle at the last minute, but the nicest treatment for cauliflower I know.

Cauliflower polonaise

Vegetables

• Easy if you don't mind doing several cooking operations at once
• 45 minutes total preparation and cooking
Serves: 4 as a first course or 6 as a side dish (in which case bacon can be omitted)

2 eggs
800g/1¾lb cauliflower (or 500g/1lb 2oz cauliflower florets)
1 tbsp oil
115g/4oz bacon rashers, thinly cut
50g/2oz white bread (about 2 medium slices) – made into crumbs either by rubbing or whizzing in a liquidiser
small handful of parsley
1 lemon
25g/1oz butter, if serving as a first course
salt and freshly ground black pepper

1. Warm a large shallow ovenproof serving dish in a low oven. Put salted water on to boil for the cauliflower. In another pan, put on the eggs to boil: when the water comes to the boil, time 10 minutes to hardboil. Trim the cauliflower and cut into quite small florets.

2. Put the oil and bacon in a frying pan and heat. Cook until crisp and put in the serving dish. Return to the oven. Do not discard the bacon fat.

3. When the cauliflower water boils, put in the florets and boil for 7–10 minutes (cauliflower is extremely variable I find). Meanwhile, put the crumbs in the reserved bacon fat and fry for 7–10 minutes, until golden – watching like a hawk and tossing frequently.

4. Meanwhile shell and chop the eggs and the parsley.

5. Assemble the salad. Drain the cauliflower and arrange in the hot serving dish with the crisp bacon. Sprinkle with the egg, then the breadcrumbs, then the parsley.

6. If serving as a first course, heat the butter to boiling and meanwhile squeeze half the lemon for its juice. Put the hot salad on hot plates, and at the last minute, mix the butter and lemon, season, pour over and serve. If serving as a side dish, simply accompany each portion with a lemon quarter.

Chopped hardboiled egg is a classic French garnish – here it adds colour and depth of flavour to a distinctive dish

Tip: *The older a cauliflower is, the longer it takes to cook through. Though it's disappointing to have to go on cooking it long after its time is up, the important thing is to ensure it's tender.*

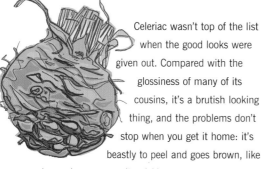

Celeriac wasn't top of the list when the good looks were given out. Compared with the glossiness of many of its cousins, it's a brutish looking thing, and the problems don't stop when you get it home: it's beastly to peel and goes brown, like apples, unless you use it quickly.

Having said all this, I do hope you'll try it, or if you've used it before and not got along with it, have another go. Winter vegetables can get pretty dull, and I would hate to be without celeriac to ring the changes; it is also top value – in winter they almost give it away. You can peel it and shred it raw, with mayonnaise stirred through, to make one of the nicest winter salads.

Finally, if you haven't had it, you may wonder what it tastes like. It is a bit like celery, but far milder. It has a peppery smell. And it is subtle. Give this baked version a go to enjoy it to its full.

1. Preheat oven to 180°C/fan oven 160°C/gas 4. Peel the celeriac and slice it thinly. Put it in a pan of salted water and bring to the boil, then boil till completely tender (about 10 minutes – but do check). Drain.
2. Put a layer in the bottom of a buttered 1.2 litre/ 2-pint dish. Dot with some of the butter, cheese, garlic and seasoning. Continue until all the celeriac is used, finishing with a layer of celeriac on top. Pour over the cream and milk, grate over a little extra cheese, dust nutmeg over all and bake undisturbed for 30–40 minutes, until puffed and golden.

Tip: *This recipe will work for practically any root vegetable – but do make sure it is fully tender at the boiling stage, as it will not soften much in the oven.*

Although no blushing beauty, celeriac has its charms

Celeriac dauphinoise

Vegetables

- Easy
- 15 minutes to prepare
- 30–40 minutes to cook
Serves: 4–6
- As a vegetable accompaniment

1kg/2lb 4oz celeriac
25g/1oz butter, plus extra for the dish
25g/1oz freshly grated parmesan cheese, plus a little extra
1 clove of garlic, finely chopped
142ml carton of single cream
3 tbsp milk
nutmeg
salt and freshly ground black pepper

This very simple autumn-winter treat was requested by a reader who was unable to capture the wonderful flavour of a batch of potato cakes she ate some years ago. I know how evocative a remembered taste can be, and I hope that this recipe touched the right nostalgic tastebud.

The reader added that the remembered potato cakes had included a measure of pastry mix – which is of course nothing more than flour and fat. Fond as I am of shortcuts, I think it is just as easy to use real ingredients, as here.

Irish potato cakes

- Can't go wrong
- 30 minutes to prepare
- 10–15 minutes to cook
Serves: 4
- Can be frozen before frying

3–4 medium baking potatoes
2 tbsp butter
2 tbsp flour
3 tbsp oil, bacon fat or butter, to fry

1. Boil the baking potatoes, scrubbed but unpeeled, in salted water until tender. Drain and slip off the skins.
2. Mash well, season to taste and beat in the butter and flour. Roll out on a floured board to just over 1cm/½-inch thick, then use a floured cutter to cut into 8cm/3-inch diameter discs.
3. Fry in the hot fat for about 3 minutes each side, until golden. Traditionally in Ireland these are served with bacon and eggs. You can also roll them out more thinly (about ½cm/¼-inch), fry for the same length of time and serve with melted butter.

Tip: *Chefs usually use this potato boiling technique – I find it excellent and easy for many dishes, though if I'm in a hurry I pull off the skins using rubber gloves.*

Inviting comfort food

You can buy fresh spinach all year round nowadays, and in the winter and spring – if you are lucky – you can find bags of pre-washed baby spinach. This is tender and flavoursome, and does not even need picking over, so is well worth the extra you will be asked to spend on it.

1. Wash the spinach leaves well. Drain them – but don't worry if they are still pretty wet – and pack into a large saucepan. Put a close fitting lid on top and cook for 2–3 minutes, shaking the pan occasionally until the leaves are wilted. Turn into a colander and drain really thoroughly, pressing down on the spinach. Leave in the colander while you proceed.

2. Heat the oil in the same pan and cook the pinenuts for 1–2 minutes until just starting to colour, moving around often so they cook evenly. Add the garlic and chilli, if using, and cook for a further minute until the nuts are golden. Stir in the raisins and drained spinach and cook about 30 seconds or so just to heat through. Season generously with salt and pepper and serve.

Tip: *The entire secret of success with spinach – and indeed much vegetable cookery – is to dry it thoroughly after cooking. This especially goes for cabbage, cauliflower and spinach, all of which can continue to leak after you've apparently drained them completely. My solution is to leave the vegetable draining in a colander right until the time you serve it. I usually put a butter paper on the surface of the veg, then the lid from the pan, which keeps it hot.*

A tasty treatment for baby spinach leaves – or indeed any spinach

Italian-style spinach

- Easy
- 10 minutes to prepare
- 10 minutes to cook

Serves: 4

500g/1lb 2oz fresh young spinach
2 tbsp olive oil
3 tbsp pinenuts
2 cloves of garlic, finely chopped
1 red chilli, seeded and chopped, optional
3 tbsp seedless raisins, roughly chopped
salt and freshly ground black pepper

This new approach to roast potatoes is offered with humility, as I realise each cook has his or her own special signature method. My mother, for instance, produces large crisp soft-centred potatoes of exceeding excellence; others prefer small and crisp. This method has a great deal to offer – and conveniently, there's no parboiling required. It works just as well with other woody herbs, such as sage or thyme.

Mediterranean roast potatoes

Vegetables

- No trouble
- 1 hour cooking

Serves: 4 (they go down well)

4 large potatoes (baking potatoes are fine) not peeled, not parboiled
3 tbsp oil
1 onion, sliced
2 cloves of garlic, thinly sliced
8 sprigs of rosemary
sea salt

1. Preheat the oven to 220°C/fan oven 200°C/gas 7 – or if roasting a joint, whatever temperature you prefer. Wash the potatoes and cut into giant chips (about 6 per potato).

2. Heat the oil in a large roasting dish. Put all the ingredients, except the sea salt, in the dish and turn them to coat with oil. Roast either in the centre of the oven or on the shelf below the meat. Every 10–15 minutes turn the vegetables with a spatula.

3. After 30 minutes turn the heat down to 200°C/fan oven 180°C/gas 6 (or according to your roasting temperature). The potatoes will be cooked in an hour. Pick out any burnt sprigs of rosemary, season generously with crushed sea salt and serve.

Slice each potato into giant-size chips – they will cook through beautifully without parboiling

Ratatouille is normally no picnic to make: hours of simmering and stirring over a hot stove when you could be doing something much more productive and/or relaxing. I hope therefore that you'll appreciate this new version, in which the vegetables are roasted 90s-style in a very hot oven, then simply given a tomato touch with those wonderful cartons of passata (tomato pulp) you can find nowadays near the canned tomatoes or pasta sauces in the supermarket.

Incidentally, when you've got your oven full on as it is here, it makes sense to make a double batch and freeze one.

1. Preheat the oven to 220°C/fan oven 210°C/gas 7. Take a large roasting tin and add half the oil. When preparing the vegetables, aim for a wide variety of shapes, and cut the ones that cook more slowly more thinly. Thus slice the onion finely, de-seed and slice the peppers thickly, slice the aubergine thickly, slice the celery into thick slices, the courgette into thick slices, cut the fennel into fine rings, slice the garlic, chop the chilli and sprinkle with the rosemary, oregano and bay leaves. Mix it all up with your hands, season well and drizzle with remaining oil. Roast for 50 minutes, turning a couple of times, until brown and tender.
2. Mix in the passata, return to the oven for 10 minutes and serve sprinkled with fresh parsley or oregano, chopped or basil, torn into pieces.

Tip: *Instead of the courgettes, you can use a small marrow, skinned, seeded and cut into chunks.*

The vegetable glut is transformed into a gluttonous treat

Roasted ratatouille

- Really easy
- 30 minutes to prepare
- 1 hour to cook
Serves: 8
- Freezes well

4 tbsp olive oil
1 large onion
2 red peppers
1 aubergine
2 sticks of celery
3 courgettes (see tip)
2 bulbs of fennel
3 cloves of garlic
1 dried red chilli
3 sprigs of rosemary
2 tsp dried, or 1 tbsp freshly
    chopped oregano
3 bay leaves
500g/1lb 2oz carton of passata
    (sieved tomatoes)
fresh herbs, such as parsley,
    oregano or basil, to serve
salt and freshly ground black
    pepper

You may remember a rather dire thing that went under this name from your schooldays: mushy cubes of potato and carrot in salad cream. This is rather different, a pleasant medley of cooked winter vegetables folded through a sour cream sauce enriched with hard-boiled egg yolk.

Real Russian salad

- Easy
- 15 minutes to prepare
- 20 minutes cooking
Serves: 4
- Can be prepared ahead

3 medium potatoes (waxy ones are best)
4 medium carrots
3 sticks of celery
1 leek
115g/4oz fresh green beans
2 eggs
150ml/¼ pint soured cream or crème fraîche
paprika
salt and freshly ground black pepper

1. Timing is of the essence. Bring a large pan of salted water to the boil. Peel the potatoes and halve; scrape the carrots; trim and halve the celery; wash and halve the leek; trim the green beans. Wash the eggs and prick the shells for hard boiling.

2. Add the potatoes and carrots to the by-now boiling water and set your timer. After 10 minutes of boiling add the eggs. After a further 3 minutes add the leek, beans and celery. After a further 5 minutes (total 18 minutes) remove all from the heat. Check all contents are tender (except the eggs – you'll have to take those on trust) and drain. Immediately immerse all in cold water to set colour and prevent further cooking.

3. When cold, dice all vegetables finely and lightly fold together. To make the sauce, shell the eggs, discard the whites (or give them to the dog) and mash the egg yolks with the cream. Add plenty of seasoning. Fold into the vegetables and serve sprinkled with paprika.

Tip: *The eggs can of course be hardboiled separately. The shells do need to be washed and there is a faint risk the eggs may crack in the boiling water, though this is lessened if you prick the blunt end first, and I haven't been caught out yet.*

A hearty mix of mainly root vegetables are bound in a sour cream dressing

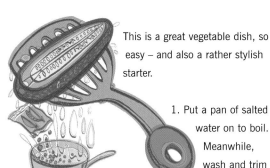

This is a great vegetable dish, so easy – and also a rather stylish starter.

See which way the courgettes will lie flat and halve them accordingly, or they'll be rolling all over your grill pan

1. Put a pan of salted water on to boil. Meanwhile, wash and trim but do not peel the courgettes. Halve them lengthwise. Boil for 5–7 minutes, covered, until neither crisp nor soft, but tender when tested with a knife.

2. Remove the courgettes from the pan with a slotted spoon (don't drain the pan) and put upside down to drain and cool. Add the frozen peas to the pan and boil for 3 minutes until beginning to go soft (in other words, slightly overcooked).

3. Whizz the salami or pancetta in the liquidiser or food processor. Add the peas, half the parmesan and the crème fraîche. Season well.

4. Using a teaspoon, scoop the seedy part out of the courgette, leaving a thick boat shape (not too much or you will be left with just a shell). Dry with kitchen paper and season, then spoon in some of the pea mixture until pleasantly heaped. Top with the rest of the parmesan.

5. Put under a preheated grill for 5–7 minutes, or until nicely golden.

Tip: *Frozen peas make a great ingredient. Gary Rhodes mashes them into potato to make a brilliant pistachio-green purée, and they also make an excellent quick soup or even sauce.*

Stuffed courgettes

- Easy
- 20 minutes to prepare
- 10 minutes to grill
- Can be made well in advance and grilled at the last minute

Ingredients per Person
1 medium courgette
65g/2½oz frozen peas
1 slice of salami, pancetta or
    other dry-cured ham
2 tbsp parmesan, freshly grated
1 tbsp crème fraîche
salt and freshly ground black
    pepper

Here's a very quick, very good vegetable accompaniment, specially suited to cold ham, hot ham or fried chicken. I have tried several different recipes to find the lightest and tastiest, and although quite fragile in the pan, this is by far the nicest.

I love sweetcorn in any form, although if it is on the cob I have to rush away for a session with the dental floss between courses. No such problem here.

Sweetcorn fritters

Vegetables

- Quick and impressive
- 5 minutes to prepare
- 15 minutes to cook
Makes 8; serves 4:
- Not for reheating

150ml/¼ pint sunflower oil,
   for shallow frying
340g tin of sweetcorn kernels
4 tbsp double cream (extra-
   thick is best) or full-fat
   crème fraîche
2 tbsp self-raising flour
pinch of sugar
salt and freshly ground black
   pepper

1. Heat a large non-stick frying pan and pour in the oil. Heat until just smoking. Meanwhile (but keeping an eye on the stove) drain the corn (open tin and, holding contents in with the lid, drain liquid into sink) and put in a bowl. Mix in the cream, then the flour, some seasoning and a good pinch of sugar.
2. Drop spoonfuls of the mixture into the oil, four at a time. Flatten slightly with a spatula to spread them a little (they should look slightly lacy) and fry for 3 minutes a side, until golden. (Flip them over with the help of two spatulas.) Don't get a shock if they pop a bit. Remove the fragile fritters to a serving dish and repeat until all the batter is used.

Tip: *Fritters are the best way of adding sparkle to leftover vegetables. Use this idea also for broccoli, cut up small, or peas.*

Don't get a shock if the fritters pop a bit as they get hot

Desserts

The days when a meal wasn't complete without a pudding are long gone, and many people now only push out the boat when entertaining. I think this is a pity, as desserts can be so creative. This chapter contains some recipes that make the most of seasonal fruits, plus some impressive ideas that are sure to end a menu with a wow.

This is a recipe for late summer, when you can go hedgerowing for this utterly fragrant and delicate dessert. If you live very remotely you may not be able to buy mascarpone, in which case use either a 142ml carton of double cream, whipped, or a 125g pack of cream cheese, beaten soft. Or if you live in the South West, clotted cream.

Blackberry shortbread tartlets

Desserts

- Easy
- 30 minutes preparation
- 10–15 minutes to bake
Serves: 6
- Pastry bases keep for up to a week in a tin; assemble maximum 1 hour before serving

For the Shortbread
100g/4oz butter, softened
¼ tsp vanilla extract
40g/1½oz icing sugar
140g/5oz self-raising flour
25g/1oz cornflour
2 tbsp ground almonds
1 egg yolk plus 2 tbsp cold water

To Finish
250g/9oz carton of mascarpone
225g/8oz blackberries
icing sugar, for dusting

1. Preheat the oven to 180°C/fan oven 160°C/gas 4. Make the shortbread: cream the butter, vanilla and sugar. Lightly mix in the flour, cornflour and almonds, then add the egg yolk and water to bind, as if you were making pastry. This can easily be done in a food mixer or food processor.

2. Find a basin or bowl with a 11cm/4¼-inch diameter rim. Roll the shortbread out very thinly (about ½ cm thick) on a well-floured board and cut round the basin with a small sharp knife to make discs. Gather the trimmings and repeat. You should have six with minimal wastage.

3. Put on two ungreased baking sheets. Prick each disc 15 times with a fork and bake for 10–12 minutes or a little longer, until pale gold.

4. Allow to cool on the tray for 2 minutes, then carefully transfer with a palette knife to a wire rack to finish cooling.

5. Before serving, beat the mascarpone to soften and spread it generously on the shortbread discs. Now scatter generously with the blackberries and at the last minute dust very generously with icing sugar.

Scatter the blackberries on to the mascarpone topping for a naturalistic effect

Tip: *Handle the dough as little as possible, and be gentle when gathering trimmings for re-rolling.*

This recipe was generously disclosed by Express reader Francis Emmorey of Kent; Canadian butter tart is quite unknown in this country, and I'd never even heard of it until that moment.

If you imagine an ultra-light, ultra-scrumptious treacle tart you will be getting somewhere near the result. I strongly advise you to try this next time you're looking for a really fine dessert.

1. Make the pastry in the usual way and line a shallow loose-bottomed 23cm/9-inch flan tin. Bake blind by lining with foil and baking beans and baking at 190°C/fan oven 170°C/gas 5 for 17 minutes, then 5 more minutes uncovered.

2. For the filling, cream the butter and add the sugar, then eggs, syrup and cream. Roughly chop the pecans and mix into the batter. If using a processor chop by hand, then whizz in briefly so they don't get over-chopped. Transfer to the baked pastry case and bake in an oven preheated to 180°C/fan oven 160°C/gas 4 for 20–30 minutes. The filling should be lightly set (it will set a little more as it cools, but you do not want it runny in the middle). Cool before removing from the pan.

Variations: *Mr Emmorey omits the nuts when he makes this. Instead he suggests:*
• soaking 100g/4oz raisins or sultanas for 24 hours in enough brandy or rum to cover and then stirring into batter before baking
• boiling 300ml/½ pint maple syrup until it is reduced to 100ml/3½fl oz, cooling and then using instead of golden syrup.

Unless you're from Canada, you've never tasted anything so good

Canadian butter pecan tart

• Not difficult
• 30 minutes to prepare
• 50 minutes to cook
Serves: 8

25g/1oz self-raising flour
140g/5oz plain flour
90g/3½oz butter
pinch of salt
2–3 tbsp cold water

For the Filling
85g/3oz butter
140g/5oz light muscovado sugar
2 eggs, well beaten
100g/4oz golden syrup
2 tbsp cream
100g/4oz pack of pecan nuts

This is so easy to make that if you've a child about the house you could make it together – no cooking required, but cream to whip, allspice to sniff, orange zest to grate.

Choc chip log

- No cooking
- 15 minutes to assemble

Serves: 8
- Can be prepared a day ahead

1 orange – a large one if
    serving children
2 tbsp Cointreau or Grand
    Marnier (adults only) or
    another orange
284ml double cream
½ tsp ground allspice
150g pack of choc chip biscuits
    – Boasters hazelnut and
    chocolate chip are specially
    good
a little chocolate, for grating

1. Choose a serving dish that will comfortably accommodate the biscuits stacked in a row.
2. Grate the zest of the orange and squeeze out the juice. Mix together. Add either the juice of a second orange (not the zest) or the liqueur.
3. Lightly whip the cream with the allspice (see tip).
4. Take a biscuit, dip quickly in the juice mixture (not for too long or it will go soggy) and then put a teaspoon of cream on it. Sandwich with another biscuit dipped in the orange and put on their side to get the log going. Continue until all biscuits are used. Don't worry if you haven't used all the juice.
5. Spoon the remaining cream over and rough up with a fork. Neaten round the outside with a piece of kitchen paper and sprinkle with a little grated chocolate.

Tip: *Don't overwhip your cream – it will thicken as you assemble the log*

A crunchy, chocolatey creation to make on a rainy afternoon

This bitter chocolate dessert is flavoured with Kahlua, the coffee liqueur, and does not involve eggs, which are such a palaver when it comes to mousse making. My mother, who as regular readers know blind-tests and quality-controls every Clever Cook recipe, came up with the idea of decorating it with those lovely chocolate matchsticks known as Matchmakers. Conveniently these come in several flavours, so if you use a different liqueur choose accordingly.

1. Choose a serving dish with a good 600ml/1 pint capacity.
2. Put the chocolate, liqueur and butter into a small pan, and stand this in a large pan full of hot water. The water should not actually boil. Stir often until melted – about 3 minutes. Take off the heat. (Alternatively melt the chocolate in the microwave on medium power for one minute.)
3. It is important now to watch your cream carefully. Put the whipping cream in a large bowl or food mixer bowl and whip until starting to become stiff – not fully whipped. Gradually whip in the chocolate mixture and continue whipping until the mixture is stiff. Pour into the dish and chill for 2–24 hours.
4. Before serving, decorate with the matchsticks, dust over a little cocoa and pour on some double cream, if desired.

Tip: *This is a brilliant dessert for large parties – when I first encountered it the host had made enough for 50.*

Place the chocolate matchsticks like the spokes of a wheel

Chocolate and kahlua mousse

Desserts

- Easy
- 15 minutes to make
- 2–24 hours chilling time
- **Serves: 4–6**
- Can be frozen

100g/4oz best dark chocolate (for instance, Sainsbury's Continental, with 70% cocoa butter content)
50ml/2fl oz (or one miniature bottle) Kahlua liqueur (or Cointreau, crème de menthe or other favourite liqueur)
25g/1oz butter
425ml/¾ pint whipping cream
a little cocoa, to finish
chocolate matchsticks
142ml double cream (not extra thick), to serve (if you wish)

Guests will be mystified by this rich, slightly sticky pudding, and as it is almost embarrassingly simple to make you might wish to keep the secret to yourself.

This recipe contains partly-cooked egg.

Coffee hedgehog pudding

Desserts

- Very easy
- 10 minutes active preparation, 6 hours chilling, 12 minutes cooking

Serves: 8

- Can be made well in advance or frozen, but add the cream and nut topping at last minute

100g/4oz butter
100g/4oz sugar
200ml/7fl oz strong freshly made coffee
1 egg, beaten
100g/4oz ground almonds
125g/4½oz Rich Tea biscuits (14 biscuits) or Marie biscuits (22 biscuits)
50g/2oz whole blanched almonds
284ml carton of double cream
50ml/2fl oz (or one miniature bottle) Kahlua or Tia Maria (coffee liqueur)

1. Melt the butter and sugar in the coffee in a medium pan. Cool slightly, stir in the egg and heat for 1–2 minutes: it will start to thicken slightly – do not boil.

2. Add the ground almonds and break in the biscuits. Mix and leave for 10 minutes. Meanwhile line a 600ml/1-pint pudding basin with a piece of clingfilm.

3. Turn the pudding into the lined basin, allow to cool and then chill for at least 6 hours.

4. Split each whole almond with a small sharp serrated knife. Toast the almonds for 5–7 minutes under a grill, or if you're of a nervous disposition for 7 minutes in a 180°C/gas 4 oven; in either case turn the nuts frequently.

5. Before the meal, invert the pudding on a serving dish (run a knife round the inside of the basin if necessary to loosen) and peel away the clingfilm. Whip the cream with the liqueur till stiff and spoon over the pudding. Decorate with the nuts, stuck in hedgehog style.

Tip: *You can now buy packets of pre-toasted flaked almonds. They're great if you're in a rush (use half the weight above or you'll be there all night sticking them in) but splitting and toasting your own gives a much nicer finish.*

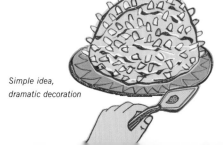

Simple idea, dramatic decoration

This is the most elegant of steamed puddings, and based on the unfortunately-named French pudding "nègre en chemise" (literally, "negro in a nightshirt"). My recipe is adapted from Jennie Reekie's jolly good *Ultimate Chocolate Cookbook* (sadly out of print).

1. Butter a 850ml/1½-pint pudding basin and line the bottom with a disc of baking parchment. Crumble the bread into the cream and leave to soak. Melt the chocolate over hot water.

2. In a mixer or food processor, cream the butter and sugar. Add everything except the eggs and mix till smooth, then break in the eggs one by one and mix till glossy. Turn into the basin and cover with a disc of baking parchment and foil, securing with a strong rubber band (see tip) or string.

3. Steam or boil for 1½ hours, topping up water as necessary.

4. Slit the vanilla bean and scrape out the seeds. Add the seeds to the cream and whip until stiff but not dry. If using the egg white (which will lighten the cream to an almost celestial fluffiness), whisk until stiff, folding in the sugar towards the end. If not using the egg white, simply fold the sugar into the cream.

5. Unmould the pudding on to a plate, sift over the icing sugar to give a snowy mantle and serve with the cream.

Tip: *My postman obligingly delivers my letters every day encircled by a strong rubber band – ideal for keeping the paper on the basin.*

Sprinkle the pudding with a cloud of icing sugar and serve with vanilla cream

French steamed chocolate pudding

Desserts

- Easy
- 20 minutes to prepare
- 1½ hours to boil
Serves: 6
- Can be prepared ahead

100g/4oz white bread, crusts off
142ml double cream (half a large carton)
50g/2oz plain chocolate
100g/4oz butter
85g/3oz sugar
50g/2oz ground almonds
4 eggs

For the Crème Chantilly
1 vanilla bean
142ml double cream (the other half of the large carton)
1 egg white, optional
1 tbsp icing sugar, plus a little extra for dusting

Fallen chocolate cake

- Trouble-free
- 20 minutes to prepare
- 30 minutes to cook,
15 minutes cooling

Serves: 8

100g/4oz unsalted butter, plus
a little extra
4 tsp cocoa, for dusting the
cake tin
200g/8oz best-quality dark
chocolate, broken up
4 large eggs, plus one extra
yolk
1 tsp vanilla extract
¼ tsp salt
100g/4oz caster sugar, or
golden caster sugar –
which I prefer
2 tbsp plain flour
a little extra cocoa, for dusting
whipped cream, to serve

I love everything about this trendy American dessert cake, even the name, which has a wonderful dramatic quality about it. In case you're wondering, it hasn't fallen from grace, or fallen in the sense of a fallen woman, but merely gently collapsed after cooking. This gives the cake a fantastic soft and melting texture, and it is meant to be very soft, semi-cooked in fact, in the centre.

This was such a success in my family that my mother made it several times, sometimes using milk chocolate (for my niece and nephew, who find plain a bit intense) – which also worked perfectly.

1. Preheat oven to 190°C/fan oven 170°C/gas 5. Butter a 20cm/8-inch springform cake tin thoroughly and dust generously with the sifted cocoa. Melt the butter gently with the chocolate in a wide pan, stirring once or twice, and set aside to cool.

2. Beat the eggs, yolk, vanilla, salt and sugar at a high speed in a mixer or with an electric hand whisk for 5 minutes or 10 minutes respectively, until smooth and mousse-like, and the mixture drops unctuously from the beaters. Scrape out of the bowl on to the melted chocolate, then sprinkle the flour on to the egg mixture and fold all together till smooth. Be patient, this takes a couple of minutes. Pour into the cake tin.

3. Bake for 27–30 minutes, until the cake is slightly cracked and has a thin crust but is still wobbly at centre. Do not continue to cook till firm, – the cake is meant to be undercooked. Cool the cake for 15 minutes, run a knife round the edge and remove the pan sides. Sift over some extra cocoa and serve warm, with extra cream.

Tip 1: *The mixture can also be baked in eight 150ml/¼-pint ramekins, in which case raise the temperature to 200°C/fan oven 180°C/gas 6 and bake on a baking sheet for 12 minutes. Turn out when cool.*

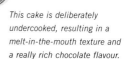

This cake is deliberately undercooked, resulting in a melt-in-the-mouth texture and a really rich chocolate flavour.

Tip 2: *If preparing ahead, make the recipe to the end of step 2 and refrigerate for up to 8 hours. Bring out of the fridge half an hour before continuing. The cake can also wait in its tin for up to 2 hours before unmoulding.*

This is dedicated to everyone who loves lemon meringue pie, but dreams of a version that is lighter, fluffier and has a lot more style.

Heavenly pie

- Worth the trouble
- Make ahead
- 20 minutes preparation
- 1½ hours to bake, 12–24 hours chilling

Serves: 6–8 (guests tend to have seconds)

For the Meringue
¼ tsp cream of tartar
175g/6oz caster sugar
4 egg whites

For the Filling
4 egg yolks
85g/3oz caster sugar
grated rind and juice of a large lemon
pinch of salt
600ml/1 pint double, whipped or whipping cream
strawberries or other fruit, or grated chocolate to garnish

1. Preheat the oven to 140°C/fan oven 125°C/gas 1. Draw a circle on a sheet of baking parchment with a pencil and turn upside-down (so the pencil doesn't come off on the meringue) and put on a baking sheet much as if making a pavlova. Make the meringue by mixing the sugar and cream of tartar – it is this that will stop the meringue setting hard, (which you don't want). Whip the egg whites till stiff, then slowly whisk in the sugar mixture till stiff and glossy.

2. Pile on to the paper and make a deep wide hollow in the middle, a sort of shallow bowl shape – the base about 1cm/½ inch thick, the rim 2–3cm/1 inch thick. Make some attractive little flick-ups round the rim. Bake for 1 hour 15 minutes to 1½ hours, till pale brown and crisp to touch. Cool in a tin away from draughts, but do not be alarmed if it cracks and falls in centre – this is correct. It will also lose its crispness as it cools.

3. Mix all the filling ingredients except the cream in a bowl over boiling water. Put the timer on and in 8–10 minutes it will turn thickish and glossy – a bit like runny lemon curd. Allow to cool and fold in half the cream, whipped.

4. About 12 to 24 hours before serving, pile the lemon cream into the crust and refrigerate. At the last minute top with the rest of the cream, whipped, and garnish with sliced strawberries or other fruit or grated chocolate.

Tip: *The egg whites need to be stiff enough for you to turn the bowl upside down without accident.*

Spoon on the fluffy meringue to make a soft crust for the pie

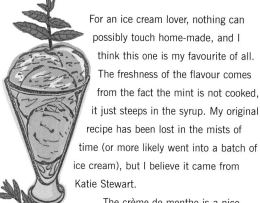

For an ice cream lover, nothing can possibly touch home-made, and I think this one is my favourite of all. The freshness of the flavour comes from the fact the mint is not cooked, it just steeps in the syrup. My original recipe has been lost in the mists of time (or more likely went into a batch of ice cream), but I believe it came from Katie Stewart.

The crème de menthe is a nice finishing touch, but can be hard to track down except at Christmas.

1. Put the sugar and water in a pan and heat slowly to dissolve, then bring to a good boil. Wash and dry the mint leaves and squeeze dry. Put the leaves in a liquidiser, cover with the hot syrup and whizz for 30 seconds, until a green slime. Return to the pan to cool thoroughly.

2. Strain into a bowl (don't press on the mint mixture) and add the remaining ingredients, mixing well. Either freeze in a metal bowl, removing to mix well after an hour and transferring to a plastic container, or in an ice cream maker.

3. If not eating at once, transfer from freezer to fridge 20 minutes before serving to soften. Garnish with sprigs of fresh mint if you haven't entirely stripped your plants.

Tip: *For mint choc chip, add Bournville chocolate, chopped quite chunkily, to the mixture when nearly frozen. (If this is for children, omit the crème de menthe.) I find Bournville best for ices as the posh 70% cocoa solids chocolate that is so good for baking is not sweet enough in a frozen state.*

An ice cream with the ring of confidence

Mint ice cream

Desserts

- Worth the trouble
- 10 minutes to prepare
- 5 minutes to cook, plus freezing time

Serves: 6

100g/4oz caster sugar
150ml/¼ pint water
1 teacupful of mint leaves, stripped from the stem (about 10g/½oz)
juice of half a lemon
284ml carton of double cream
2 tbsp crème de menthe or mint syrup, optional

Jane Tucker's Christmas pudding

- 45 minutes preparation
- 8 hours boiling or steaming
- **2-pint pudding serves 12, 1-pint serves 6, ½-pint serves 4**
- well wrapped, puddings keep comfortably for a year

50g/2oz blanched almonds, chopped
2 large apples, peeled, and cored and chopped
200g/8oz citron peel, chopped
125g/4½oz plain flour
125g/4½oz soft white breadcrumbs
250g/9oz box of beef suet
1kg/2lb 4oz stoned raisins (four boxes)
100g/4oz soft brown sugar – crumble if it looks lumpy
¾ nutmeg, grated
3 eggs, beaten
2 tbsp brandy

This should be made on the Sunday late in November known as Stir-up Sunday, so called after its collect ("Stir up, we beseech thee, O Lord, the wills of thy faithful people…"). My recipe is a late Victorian one given to me by Susannah Mudge of Chulmleigh, Devon.

There is a family legend attached to it. Jane Tucker's daughter Josephine was a contralto with D'Oyly Carte. One Christmas, probably about 1920, the company lunched at the Savoy, and when Josephine's young son was asked how he liked the pudding, he replied: "Not as good as my grandmother's!"

I have edited the recipe so that you're not left with any annoying ends of packets. Ingredients for all three puds total about £8 – less than you'd pay for one this fine in the shops.

1. Get everything prepared. The almonds and apples can be chopped in a processor, but the citron peel must be done by hand. Mix all the ingredients together in a bowl for a good 3–4 minutes – it is ready when it subsides slightly after each stir. Ask the family to stir too, and get everyone to make a wish.

2. Prepare the pans and pudding basins. This quantity (*one quarter* of the amount made by Jane Tucker!) will make a 850ml/1½-pint pudding + 600ml/1-pint pudding + 300ml/½-pint pudding (I find these fit handily in one big pan plus one oval casserole). Butter the basins well and pack in the mixture to within 2.5cm/1 inch of the top. Cover with a double layer of greaseproof paper or baking paper, pleated to allow for expansion and tied with string (keep the paper in place with a rubber band while tying). Then wrap with one layer of aluminium foil brought right up from the bottom over the top, and another right over and under. Tie with more string, and if the basin is a tight fit in its pan, make a string harness to help it in and out.

3. Steam or boil for 8 hours, topping up with water as necessary. Cool overnight. On Christmas Day boil for 1 hour.

Tip 1: *When cooled, discard the rather messy wrappings around the puddings and rewrap in spanking new greaseproof, foil and string.*
Tip 2: *Serve this with tutti frutti brandy butter. To make, cream 175g/6oz unsalted butter with the rind of half an orange and 4 tbsp icing sugar. Gradually beat in 4 tbsp brandy or cognac and finely chopped crystallised fruit (use 6 glacé cherries, a small piece of crystallised angelica and a small piece of crystallised ginger, or stem ginger in syrup – or fruits of your choice). Put in a small bowl, fork over the top attractively and leave to set in fridge.*

A really fine old-fashioned pud

This recipe was inspired by a friend, Jacqueline Lewin, who invariably produces (from the tiniest kitchen you have ever seen) the most imaginative and creative feasts. Like many of the best things in life, it is astonishingly simple, and the only requirement is that the nectarines should be ripe and the dish should be eaten while still warm from the oven.

The vanilla is important. Vanilla extract is a very different thing from vanilla essence, which is artificially manufactured and tastes it. Although the extract seems expensive it makes a real difference to everything it touches (see Mocha praline gâteau, page 86)

Vanilla pods are even further up the gourmet scale. Keep these in a jar of caster sugar to give it a light perfume (I still recommend adding extract in recipes, though, for a full flavour) and for special dishes, slit the pods and scrape out and use the fudgy black seeds. These need no further preparation – just add them to creams and custards to give a faint speckle and luscious flavour.

Nectarines in mascarpone

Desserts

- Very easy
- 10 minutes preparation (can be done in advance)
- 10 minutes baking

Serves: 4

- Serve warm from the oven (do not reheat)

250g/9oz carton of mascarpone
1 tsp vanilla extract, not essence
2 tbsp sugar
1 tbsp marsala or sherry
3 ripe, juicy nectarines, sliced thinly (not peeled)
almond biscuits, to serve

1. Up to 12 hours in advance, mix the first four ingredients in a bowl till creamy. Fold in the nectarines thoroughly but gently. Put into a shallow dish of about 850ml/1½-pint capacity and refrigerate until ready to bake.
2. Preheat oven to 180°C/fan oven 180°C/gas 4. Just before serving, put in the oven for 10 minutes but watch carefully and remove the minute the mascarpone starts to bubble (otherwise it will become grainy). Serve warm at once with almond biscuits.

Slice the nectarines thinly – they do not need peeling

This is something amazing to keep up your sleeve. It is the very best sort of emergency pudding for a dinner party – fabulous flavour, extravagant and so impressive. All you need to serve is some double cream.

One important point: unripe peaches are murder to skin. Try scalding and skinning just one at first and if it won't go, make this recipe when the peaches have ripened.

1. Find one 1-litre, or two ½-litre preserving jars that will accommodate the fruit. Sterilise the jar or jars by washing well, draining thoroughly and laying in an oven at 150°C/fan oven 130°C/gas 2 for 15 minutes. If using rubber seals, it is always best to use new ones, carefully washed.

2. Bring a large pan of water to the boil and remove from the heat. Two by two, slip in the peaches for 2 minutes, then remove to a bowl of cold water with a spoon, spear with a fork and peel off the skin with a small sharp knife. Bring the water back to the boil between skinnings. Keep the peaches whole.

3. Dissolve the sugar in 300ml/½ pint water and bring to a slow boil. Simmer the peaches for 5 minutes. Transfer to the jar or jars with a slotted spoon. Measure 150ml/¼ pint of the syrup into a small pan and add the brandy. Bring to the boil and pour over the peaches till overflowing. Seal the jars and keep cool and dark: eat within 8 weeks.

Tip: *You will have about 300ml/½ pint syrup left over. Keep this in the fridge and use for fruit salads, poaching fruit and so on.*

Summer sunshine captured for later in the year

Peaches in brandy

Desserts

- Straightforward but requires care
- 30 minutes to prepare
- 10 minutes to cook
Serves: 6
- Keeps for 8 weeks

8 peaches, weighing about
   1kg/2lb 4oz
350g/12oz granulated sugar
150ml/¼ pint brandy

Lady Hornby's soufflé

- Surprisingly easy
- 10 minutes to prepare
- 15–17 minutes to cook

Serves: 3–4

butter and caster sugar for
    the dish
3 heaped tbsp firm marmalade
1 tbsp brandy
5 large egg whites
pinch of salt
100g/4oz caster sugar
25g/1oz slivered toasted nuts –
    almonds are ideal

Custard Sauce, optional
3 egg yolks
125ml/4fl oz double cream
125ml/4fl oz milk
1 tbsp sugar
1 tsp cornflour
drop of vanilla extract or brandy

This is a simply brilliant recipe – a marmalade soufflé that needs no messing around with white sauces and egg yolks. Not only is it a doddle to make and tastes marvellous, but it doesn't collapse the way a normal soufflé does and, miraculously, it's low in fat. I owe the fact I can share it with you to the extreme generosity of my neighbour Sheran Hornby, whose parties large and small are the epitome of glamour. With a dish like this in your repertoire, it must be much more tempting to keep it under your hat.

If you don't have much luck with soufflés, or haven't dared try them, have a go at this. As long as you whip the egg whites till completely stiff (so you can turn the bowl upside down without the egg white sliding out) and fold in the marmalade patiently and gently, I can't see how anyone could go wrong.

At this point I will also make the strange confession that the only thing I can't bear to eat is marmalade (bad experience at school: I would need counselling to be able to enjoy it). Yet in this form, it is scrumptious.

I have accompanied the soufflé with a quick custard sauce (this isn't low fat) to use up some of the egg yolks, but this is by no means essential. If beginners embark on this too, note that the custard must not approach boiling, or it will curdle – but it needs to cook to thicken it. I find this takes from 10–20 minutes according to how quickly it heats.

1. Butter a 1.7-litre/3-pint soufflé dish well and sprinkle all over with sugar (this is not so much to help it rise – it makes no difference, but to give the crust extra flavour). Preheat the oven to 200°C/fan oven 180°C/gas 6. Stir the marmalade and brandy together until well mixed.

2. Whisk the egg whites for a minute with the salt. When they get stiff add the sugar and beat away until

stiff and glossy. Fold in the marmalade mixture and turn into the soufflé dish. Sprinkle with the nuts and bake for 15–17 minutes.

3. Meanwhile, make the custard. Whisk all ingredients together in a pan. Heat over another pan of simmering water till hot and slightly thickened. Taste, add a little more sugar if you like, and serve with the soufflé.

4. When the soufflé is ready, remove it from the oven and preferably serve at once; if you need to delay it, turn off the oven, open the oven door a crack and leave for 5–10 minutes and it will only slightly deflate.

Tip: *If cooking for a large dinner party, make two soufflés – don't try to put double the mixture in a dish double the size.*

The cleverest soufflé you'll ever make

Mocha praline gâteau

- Easy
- 10 minutes for the praline
- 15 minutes to assemble gâteau
- 3–4 hours setting overnight in the fridge
- Cuts into 10

For the Praline
50g hazelnuts in their skins
50g almonds in their skins
100g caster sugar

For the Gâteau
284ml carton of double cream
142ml carton of single cream
3 tbsp instant coffee, or 3 tsp Coffee Drop
2 tsp caster sugar, if using Coffee Drop
200ml milk
200g pack of sponge fingers (you will use about ¾ of the pack)

This is a lovely old-fashioned kind of dessert. The praline is home-made (a fun operation, and so simple) but the cake itself is a clever compilation of sponge fingers and cream.

There are two ways to give the gâteau its luscious coffee flavouring. The traditional way is to use instant coffee powder. Even more delectable is to use Coffee Drop, a 100% natural coffee extract all the way from Costa Rica. You can get this and also the vanilla extract I always recommend from Lakeland, Alexandra Buildings, Windermere, Cumbria LA23 1BQ. If you're not already on the Lakeland mailing list, then you should be: the only grudge I bear this admirable cookware specialist is that I offered them my Lakeland Terrier puppy (Keswick her name) as a mascot and they don't seem to have taken me up on the offer. She's still available, incidentally.

This is far easier to make in metric, so I hope even imperial cooks will have a go.

1. Make the praline. Put a piece of foil on a baking sheet. Choose a small heavy pan, not non-stick, and a strong metal or wooden spoon (plastic will melt). Put in the nuts and sugar and stir about over a medium heat (you must stir all the time from now on); the sugar will gradually melt. Keep stirring as the sugar continues to melt and the mixture gets sticky. After 3–4 minutes the mixture will brown and emit a puff of caramel vapour. Remove from the heat, check all looks good and brown and tip on to the baking sheet. Leave to set for a few minutes: hey presto, you have made nut brittle.

2. When cold and hard, snap off a few caramelised hazelnuts for decoration and pile the rest in the food processor or liquidiser. Pulverise thoroughly (the noise will frighten the cat) and for up to 2 minutes until

finely ground. Transfer to a jar; you will need about half for this recipe.

3. Oil a loose-based 18cm/7-inch cake tin. Whip the creams lightly and as the mixture stiffens beat in 2 tbsp coffee powder dissolved in 2 tbsp of the milk, warmed, or 2 tsp of the Coffee Drop, plus the sugar. Mix the remaining milk with the rest of the coffee or Coffee Drop.

4. Dip the sponge fingers generously in the coffee-milk mix to soak them well and fit a layer, cutting as necessary, on the bottom of the tin. Top with one third of the cream and 4 tbsp of praline. Repeat with another layer of sponge fingers and another one third of the cream. Leave to set for 3–4 hours.

5. Unmould, cover completely with the remaining cream and sprinkle thickly with 4 more tbsp praline and the reserved hazelnuts. Leave overnight and serve.

Tip 1: *You can if you prefer layer the dessert in a glass dish (a bit like a trifle) and leave overnight. Sprinkle praline on top to finish.*
Tip 2: *Use the remaining praline to decorate cakes or scatter on ice-cream or mousses*

Layer the biscuits neatly in the tin

Everyone who loves apple Tarte Tatin will adore this pear version. Although not quick to make, this is a sumptuous way to finish a dinner party or Sunday lunch.

Pear tarte tatin

• Requires some care, but not difficult
• 25 minutes preparation
• 1¼ hours partially attended cooking
Serves: 6
• Best served fresh

For the Pastry
pinch of salt
140g/5oz flour
85g/3oz butter, chilled and
    cubed

For the Filling
8 pears (about 900g/2lb),
    nearly but not quite ripe
50g/2oz butter
50g/2oz sugar
crème fraîche, to serve

1. Make pastry in food processor by whizzing flour, a pinch of salt and the butter till the mixture has the texture of breadcrumbs. With machine running, add 2–3 tbsp cold water. The pastry should just come together; pat gently into a ball, squash into a disc and put in the refrigerator.
2. Take a 22cm/8½-inch shallow cake tin, with a fixed bottom. Line with a disc of waxed paper; butter the sides well. Preheat oven to 220°C/fan oven 200°C/gas 7.
3. Peel the pears thinly; quarter them and remove the cores. Set to one side. Melt the second batch of butter in a large non-stick frying pan, add the pears and sugar and cook for 30–35 minutes until a really good golden brown: be patient as the flavour of the dish depends on this caramelisation process.
4. While they are cooking, roll out the pastry on a floured surface to a round to fit the tin. Don't be fretful if it isn't perfect as it will not be seen.
5. Put the pears into the tin and then, folding the pastry over the rolling pin, lift it over the pears to cover. Trim any obvious irregularities and tuck the edge down around the pears.
6. Bake for 25–30 minutes until pale brown. Loosen round the edge carefully and invert on to a plate. Tap the tin gently to release any topping that's stuck. Serve warm with crème fraîche.

Tip: *For cooking, pears are almost always better slightly under-ripe.*

This is an ingenious peach dish in which the fruit is baked with those little ratafia biscuits – the ones that are often wrapped in pretty pastel paper (though you do not need wrapped ones for this). Interestingly, the ratafia essence used to flavour these biscuits is made from peach kernels, and when you enter a really fine bakery or patisserie this is often the source of that wonderful almondy aroma.

This is a very unusual recipe in that it is equally practical for one or one hundred. In smaller quantities, you can equally well use your grill – about 5–8 minutes under a hot grill.

1. Preheat oven to 220°C/fan oven 220°C/gas 7.
2. Slice the peach in half, not as you would usually do it, from top to bottom, but across the centre (if you think of it like a globe, across the Equator). This cuts across the fruit's fibres, and adds to the succulence of the result. Sprinkle with lightly crushed ratafia, the brandy, then the sugar.
3. Bake for 5–10 minutes, until just going brown. Serve with whipped cream.

Tip: *A peach's ripeness can be difficult to judge; if in doubt another day or two will not harm it. Even those sold as "ripe and ready to eat" in the trendier supermarkets are better after being acclimatised for a couple of days, I find. To halve a peach neatly, cut carefully then twist it lightly between your hands (as if your were unscrewing one half from the other). If necessary tease the stone out of the half in which it remains with a sharp knife.*

Ratafia peaches

- Very easy
- Less than 5 minutes to prepare
- 10 minutes to cook
- Also good eaten cold
- Not for freezing

Ingredients per Person
1 firm peach
2 ratafia biscuits
2 tsp brandy
1 teaspoon brown sugar
whipped cream, to serve

A halved peach is an invitation for a delicate filling

It is said that this pudding is to the 90s what Black Forest Gâteau was to the 70s. I much prefer it, being far simpler to make, and I'm indebted to reader Mrs Caunce of Preston for sending me this recipe. I have adapted it to be steamed or boiled in a pudding basin, rather than baked; though if you would rather make a baked pudding, omit 1 tbsp of the milk and bake in a loaf tin for 45 minutes at 180°C/fan oven 160°C/gas 4 instead. (You can give the baked version a super deluxe touch by making extra sauce, splitting and spreading the pud with it before reheating and serving with more sauce).

Sticky toffee pudding

- Easy
- 30 minutes to prepare
- 1½ hours boiling
Serves: 6

85g/3oz butter
85g/3oz light muscovado sugar
   (Billington's is best)
1 egg plus 1 egg yolk
½ tsp vanilla extract
175g/6oz self-raising flour
1 tsp mixed spice
175g/6oz stoned dates, cut up
3 tbsp milk

For the Toffee Sauce
100g/4oz light muscovado
   sugar
100g/4oz butter
4 tbsp cream
¼ tsp vanilla extract

1. Butter a 850ml/1½-pint pudding basin and put a disc of baking parchment at the bottom. Put a large lidded pan or steamer on to boil. Cream the butter with the sugar and beat in the eggs and vanilla. Add the flour and spice, then the dates and milk, and stir until combined. The mixture should be slightly sloppy: turn into the basin, cover with greaseproof paper (tying tightly to prevent water getting in) and steam or boil for 1½ hours, until risen and firm.

2. Meanwhile, make the sauce: boil the first three ingredients together for 5 minutes, then add the vanilla. You can make this in advance and reheat it.

Tip: *You can buy beautiful fresh Medjool dates at many supermarkets during the winter. They are so tender and sweet it seems almost a crime to cook with them, but they make this pudding even more sumptuous.*

A rich and unctuous pud for cold days

Cakes and bakes

There is nothing more satisfying than an afternoon bake-in; shutting the kitchen door, putting on the radio and immersing yourself in something as creative and blameless as mixing up a batch of scones, biscuits, or most satisfying of all, a cake. Many readers may in fact be like me, and find they bake far more than they can actually eat. A freezer is a godsend, or better still, a network of appreciative friends who are happy to indulge this small weakness and take the extra off your hands.

Almond and coconut tuiles

- Fun to make
- 15 minutes to prepare
- 40 minutes baking and finishing
Makes: 18

75g/2½oz butter
50g/2oz caster sugar
couple of drops of vanilla
    extract
40g/1½oz plain flour
25g/1oz flaked almonds
15g/½oz desiccated coconut

Tuiles means tiles, and that is the shape these extremely fragile delicacies should form when, still hot from the oven, they are draped over a lightly oiled rolling pin or bottle (one that doesn't roll around of its own accord). Measure the ingredients carefully as the quantities are small and the proportions important.

The finished result presents a problem: the biscuits are extremely light and moreish, and a batch will disappear in no time. Yet storing them out of the sight of peckish eyes you are bound to break a few. Answer: make double what you think you'll need.

1. Heat the oven to 190°C/fan oven 170°C/gas 5. Cream butter, sugar and vanilla and stir in the flour. If you do this with a mixer, now continue by hand. Stir in the almonds and coconut till well combined.
2. Line a baking sheet with baking parchment or silicone Bake-o-Glide paper. Roll 6 teaspoonful-size balls of mixture, put on the baking sheet and flatten with a fork dipped in water. Bake for 4–5 minutes, turning after 2 minutes, until they are toasted all over, but darker round the edges. If you take them out too soon and the centre of each tuile is still pale beige they will still taste good but they will not set entirely crisply. If you let them go too brown they will shatter and be very hard to handle.
3. While they are baking, lightly oil a rolling pin and try and prop it so that it won't roll. When the biscuits are ready, leave for 1 minute on the tray to firm up a little (if you move them too soon they will fall to bits) then use a spatula to lay the first three over the rolling pin to firm up. They will harden quickly; transfer to plates (they get all snagged up if you use a cooling tray) and repeat with the rest of the batch. Repeat the whole process.

4. Serve the biscuits with ice cream. They are light as air and extremely fragile so handle carefully.

Tip 1: *Even in a fan oven the biscuits won't brown perfectly evenly.*

Tip 2: *If you leave it too long and the biscuits harden on the tray, simply reheat for 30 seconds and they will become malleable again. Do not attempt more than six at a time, even if you have a spare rolling pin.*

Tip 3: *If you don't want to cool the biscuits this way, cool on a cold flat surface, shifting after a couple of seconds to prevent sticking – not on a cooling tray, as they'll fall straight through.*

Cakes and bakes

Cool the "tiles" on a rolling pin then slide free

Slices of fresh banana give this tea bread a tropical lilt

Banana loaf

Cakes and bakes

- Easy
- 25 minutes preparation
- 1 hour to bake
- Cuts into 10 slices; keeps for several days in a tin (unless decorated with fresh banana)

250g/9oz Scofa Soda Bread flour mix
125g/5oz butter
1 egg
100g/4oz caster sugar
2 tbsp runny honey
2 tsp cinnamon
grated rind of half an orange
2 large ripe bananas, mashed up
50g/2oz walnuts, chopped
3 tbsp milk

To Finish
1 tbsp icing sugar
125g/4oz pack of Philadelphia cream cheese
25g/1oz candied banana chips (picked out from a bag of tropical fruit and nut mix) or one fresh banana, to decorate

Tea breads are not specially fashionable nowadays, which is a pity, as they're fun to make and excellent with a cup of tea or coffee. This recipe takes advantage of one of the bread mixes that you can find quite easily nowadays.

1. Preheat oven to 190°C/gas 5 (for fan ovens see Tip 1). Thoroughly grease and flour a loaf tin of 850ml/1½ pint capacity. Put the flour mix in a large bowl and rub in the butter until it resembles breadcrumbs. Mix in the egg, sugar, honey, cinnamon, orange rind, bananas and walnuts, then add the milk to make a soft consistency.

2. Turn into the tin and bake in the centre of the oven for 1 hour. Cover with foil after 40 minutes if already sufficiently brown. The loaf is cooked when it is just firm to the touch – remove from the oven and cool for 5 minutes.

3. Turn out on to a wire rack, then cool right side up. Beat the icing sugar into the cream cheese. When the loaf is quite cold, spread the top with the softened cream cheese and decorate either with banana chips or if you are intending to eat the cake all at one sitting, with fresh banana. Slice with a serrated knife (it does not need buttering).

Tip 1: *If you have a fan oven, reduce the oven temperature to 170°C, cover after 40 minutes and check progress after 55 minutes.*

Tip 2: *Greasing tins, although a bit of a fiddle, should hold no mystery. Ideally I use very soft butter, which gives a wonderful finish to the crust of whatever is being cooked, and is very easy to apply either with your hand or a piece of kitchen paper.*

There are so many different versions of this cake in existence, and I must say I never run out of enthusiasm to try a new one.

The crunch most usually associated with my neighbour Bryony is that of gravel, as she swishes off somewhere amazing in her racing green MG convertible. But her children Claire and George feel this is an even finer contribution to village life.

1. Put the butter in a pan and melt gently on the hob. When melted, break in the chocolate off the heat and stir to melt; the heat from the butter should achieve this, but if not, warm gently again, stirring constantly so it doesn't catch and burn. If you're of a very nervous disposition you can do this over a pan of very hot or gently simmering water, but it shouldn't really be necessary, and you can save yourself some washing up.
2. Stir in the sugar, egg yolks and vanilla. You do not cook the egg yolks – they are included to keep the texture soft. Smash the Nice biscuits in a plastic bag and stir into the mixture. Turn into a small (850ml/ 1½ pint capacity) loaf tin lined with foil and leave to set overnight.
3. Serve in slices, dusted with icing sugar.

Tip 1: *This recipe contains uncooked eggs, not a worry for Bryony as she keeps her own handsome hens, but for the rest of us I recommend fresh-as-possible free-range eggs.*

Tip 2: *This sets very firmly. You can make it softer, and give it an adult tang, by adding a couple of tablespoons of brandy at step 2.*

Bryony's chocolate biscuit crunch cake

- Easy; no real cooking
- 15 minutes preparation
- Overnight setting in the fridge
- Cuts into at least 8
- Keeps well, can be frozen

150g/5½oz butter
150g/5½oz high quality plain chocolate
50g/2oz sugar, either caster or light muscovado
2 egg yolks
1 tsp vanilla extract
300g/10oz pack of Nice biscuits
icing sugar, for dusting

A chocolate crunch cake with go-faster stripes

Buttermilk scones

- No problem
- 5 minutes to prepare
- 12 minutes to cook

Makes: 8–10 scones

250g self-raising flour
4 tsp baking powder
½ tsp salt
1 tbsp sugar
1 tsp cream of tartar
50g butter
150ml buttermilk, or half plain
    set yogurt, half milk
a little milk

I found this recipe in the back of a drawer, in the handwriting of a great friend. She is called Anni Bowes and nowadays livens up a rather pretty corner of Warwickshire; at the time she shared this recipe however she was something of a London raver. There are two puzzling things about it. First of all, what was Anni doing making scones in those heady King's Road days, assuming she ever found half an hour to spare between hangovers? Secondly, the slip of paper is proudly labelled up Wood Scone Supreme – who or what might Wood be or have been?

Nevertheless I tried the recipe and have never made better or lighter scones. This is incidentally a recipe to measure in metric as it involves lovely round numbers.

1. Preheat the oven to 200°C/fan oven 180°C/gas 6. Sift the first five ingredients into a large bowl. Rub in the butter till well combined. Make an indentation in the top of the crumbly mixture, pour in the buttermilk and mix until the dough comes together.
2. At this point, knead lightly until just smooth. Transfer to a floured board and roll out to 2.5cm/1 inch thick – a few strokes of the rolling pin will accomplish this. Use a 6cm/2½-inch floured metal cutter to cut out 9–10 thick discs and transfer carefully, preferably using a metal spatula so you don't smudge the sides, to a large ungreased baking sheet.
3. Brush the tops only with milk (you don't want it down the sides) and bake for 10–12 minutes, until golden brown.

Tip 1: *The dough mustn't be too wet as this will inhibit rising (as does cheese or extra fat).*

*Perky
high-rise scones*

This recipe was sent to me by Mrs Virginia Isitt of Scunthorpe, who procured it at Bangor Cathedral; the original bears the name Mair Glyndwr Williams.

When this recipe was published, I received several dozen letters from readers saying it was the best cake they had ever made – letters from all over the country, not just Wales.

1. Chop the cherries and pineapple (keep the juice). Put in a pan with the pineapple juice, butter, mixed fruit and sugar. Heat to melt the butter but do not boil. Leave to cool, then beat in the flour and eggs.

2. Preheat oven to 170°C/fan oven 150°C/gas 3. Line a 20cm/8-inch round tin with baking paper, put in mixture and bake for about 1½ hours, till firm and a skewer comes out clean.

An authentic recipe from Bangor

Cacen byth yn methu (never fail cake)

- Easy
- 40 minutes to prepare
- 1½ hours to cook
- **Cuts into 8–10**
- Freezes well

100g/4oz glacé cherries
220g tin of pineapple in juice
100g/4oz butter
350g/12oz mixed fruit
175g/6oz soft brown sugar
225g/8oz self-raising flour
2 eggs

Chocolate meringue birthday cake

- Worth the effort
- 1 hour active work
- 2 hours baking
Cuts into at least 12 slices
- Can be made a day ahead

For the Chocolate Sponge
50g/2oz plain chocolate
4 eggs
100g/4oz caster sugar
1 tbsp Chocolate Extract,
    optional (see tip)
50g/2oz plain flour
40g/1½oz cocoa powder

For the Meringue
3 egg whites
140g/5oz caster sugar
1 tbsp cocoa
100g/4oz bag of ground
    hazelnuts

For the White Chocolate Cream
200g/8oz best white chocolate
3 tbsp hot water
600ml/1 pint double cream
1 tbsp brandy
1 tsp Chocolate Extract, optional
chocolate leaves, grated
    chocolate or praline,
    to decorate

For my sister-in-law's birthday, I was delighted to divulge my all-time favourite chocolate cake recipe. It's a four-layer affair of hazelnut meringue and chocolate sponge, and rather special – but then again, so is Sharon.

1. Preheat the oven to 180°C/fan oven 160°C/gas 4. Take a 20cm/8-inch loose-based spring-form cake tin and two sheets of baking parchment: trace a circle the same size as the tin onto each piece of paper (pressing pencil in firmly) and put them upside down on baking sheets (otherwise the pencil mark will irritatingly transfer itself onto the bottom of your meringue). Line the tin with baking paper.

2. Melt the first lot of chocolate over hot water. Whisk the eggs and sugar electrically for a good 5 minutes until light and pale and the whisk leaves a trail. Fold in the chocolate plus Chocolate Extract if using, then sift in the flour and cocoa and fold in. Transfer to the tin and bake for 25–30 minutes until firm. When cold, slice the cake horizontally into two thin discs. Lower oven temperature to 110°C/fan oven 110°C/gas ¼.

3. Whisk the egg whites till stiff but not dry and add half the sugar. Continue whisking till stiff and glossy. Fold in the remaining sugar, cocoa and hazelnuts. If the cake is for a really special occasion pipe a ring just inside the circle on the paper, then spoon in the rest and level. Otherwise, just pile in and neaten at the edge.

4. Bake for 1¾–2 hours (1½ hours in fan oven). Ovens vary, especially at low temperatures and even more so when baking for such a long period, so check meringues are crisp and if necessary return to the oven upside down to finish off.

5. Melt the white chocolate with the water (if it is hot the chocolate will melt almost at once), whip the

cream till stiffening and beat in the chocolate and
brandy and the Chocolate Extract if using.

6. Then assemble the cake. Start with a meringue
layer, top with a thin layer of cream, then cake and
cream, meringue then cake. Spoon the remaining
white chocolate cream on top and round sides.
Decorate with chocolate leaves, grated chocolate or
praline. Eat at once or refrigerate until ready.

Tip: *Chocolate Extract is a*
brilliant pure cocoa essence
from the States you can get
from Lakeland – it intensifies
the flavour. Lakeland is at
Alexandra Buildings,
Windermere,
Cumbria LA23 1BQ.

Lavish layers of cake and
meringue for a special
occasion

This delightful recipe was sent in by Patricia Gregory of Prestbury, Cheltenham. Patricia writes, "Great amusement is caused when friends are invited to have a cuddle. In fact most ask for a second cuddle, and who can refuse?"

The cuddles are in fact small biscuits sandwiched together with a vanilla cream mixture; after tasting these you will never be able to look those bought custard creams in the eye again.

Custard cuddles

Cakes and bakes

- Easy
- 15 minutes to prepare
- 15 minutes to bake and finish
Makes: about 10
- Keep in a tin for 48 hours, refrigerate if you prefer a firmer filling

50g/2oz butter
50g/2oz caster sugar
½ tsp vanilla extract
1 egg yolk
25g/1oz cornflour
85g/3oz self-raising flour

For the Filling
25g/1oz butter
25g/1oz icing sugar
½ tsp vanilla extract
a little icing sugar, for dusting

1. Preheat the oven to 190°C/fan oven 170°C/gas 5. Grease two baking sheets. Cream the butter and sugar with vanilla and beat in the egg yolk. Mix in the flours until just combined. Form 18–20 small balls a bit bigger than mothballs and put on the baking sheets. Flatten slightly with a fork and bake for 8–10 minutes until just colouring – don't overbake or they'll harden. Remove from the oven and after a couple of minutes transfer to trays to cool.

2. When cool, sandwich pairs of the biscuits with a little of the filling, made by creaming the butter, icing sugar and vanilla together.

3. Sift a little icing sugar over and serve as described by Mrs Gregory.

Invite close friends round for a Custard Cuddle

Tip 1: *Icing sugar is one of the few ingredients that needs sifting. Not if being beaten into butter, but certainly for glacé or royal icing, and if being used as a decoration.*

Tip 2: *If like me you have banned vanilla essence from the kitchen and only use extract, you may find the top sticks tenaciously. Wrap a wide elastic band around the cap and you should be able to open without problem.*

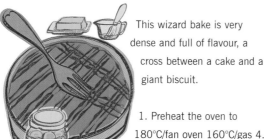

This wizard bake is very dense and full of flavour, a cross between a cake and a giant biscuit.

1. Preheat the oven to 180°C/fan oven 160°C/gas 4. Line the base of a 20cm/8-inch loose-bottomed shallow sandwich tin with baking parchment and grease the sides generously with 25g/1oz of the butter.

2. Cream the rest of the butter and sugar thoroughly (save the butter paper). Beat in the ginger, chopped finely. Add the flour, a good pinch of salt and most of the egg (saving about 1 tsp for glazing) and mix till smooth – it will be very stiff indeed.

3. Turn into the tin, and using a spatula and fork (or your hands) flatten down – the mixture will stick to the paper, but continue patiently until you have a smooth result. Add a teaspoon of water to the remaining egg and brush over the top, then mark with a fork, lattice fashion.

4. Bake on a baking sheet in the centre of the oven for 30 minutes, then cover with the butter paper and bake for a full 45 minutes more. The cake will be a rich dark golden colour; if the edges start to singe, move to a lower shelf of the oven.

5. Remove from the oven and keep the butter paper in place while you press the centre (which will have risen slightly), down firmly with an oven cloth; then leave to cool uncovered for 15 minutes or so, invert, remove tin and baking paper and leave on a rack until cold.

Tip: *I never throw away a butter paper – they have dozens of uses, from covering waiting vegetables to greasing tins and covering cakes as they brown.*

Mark the dough with a fork into a rough lattice for a professional effect

Danish ginger butter cake

Cakes and bakes

- Easy
- 15 minutes preparation
- 1¼ hours baking, 45 minutes cooling

Serves: 8
- Keeps for a week in a tin

250g/9oz pack unsalted (preferably Danish) butter
225g/8oz caster sugar
115g/4oz stem ginger (about 7 pieces)
300g/10oz plain flour
good pinch of salt
large egg, beaten

A fiendish bake for Hallowe'en or anytime you fancy something wickedly rich

Devil's food cake

- Worth the trouble
- 30 minutes to prepare
- 30 minutes to cook
- **Cuts into 8–10**
- Freezes well

40g/1½oz cocoa (not drinking chocolate)

2 tsp instant coffee powder, preferably espresso type (or 1.8g sachet)

2 tsp vanilla extract

2 tsp Coffee Drop coffee extract, optional (see page 86)

200ml/7fl oz boiling water

lard or butter for oiling the tins (see tip)

175g/6oz unsalted butter, softened

175g/6oz caster sugar

2 large eggs

175g/6oz plain flour, plus a little extra for dusting the tins

½ tsp bicarbonate of soda

½ tsp salt

For the Satanic Frosting

200g/8oz best quality plain chocolate

284ml whipping cream

2 tbsp golden syrup, or for adults, Tia Maria liqueur

A dangerously scrumptious and moist cake from the United States.

1. Put the cocoa, coffee powder, vanilla and, coffee extract (if using) in a bowl and pour over the boiling water. Whisk to dissolve, transfer to a jug and allow to cool to room temperature (about 20 minutes). Meanwhile, preheat the oven to 180°C/fan oven 160°C/gas 4.

2. Grease and flour two 22cm/8½-inch shallow sandwich tins. Cream the butter and sugar until pale and fluffy. Add one egg and beat for a minute, then the other and beat a full minute longer; if using a mixer, wipe down sides with a spatula as necessary.

3. Sift the remaining ingredients. Now beat in a third of the flour mixture, and when almost smooth add a third of the cocoa liquid. Repeat twice and beat for a minute until satiny.

4. Turn into the tins and bake for 25–30 minutes, until just firm to the touch and a toothpick inserted in the centre comes out with just a crumb or two sticking to it. Cool for 10 minutes and turn out.

5 To make the frosting, whizz the chocolate in a food processor till sandy (this is noisy). Bring the cream to the boil and pour over the chopped chocolate with the machine running, then add golden syrup or Tia Maria. Transfer to a bowl – it thickens as it cools and can be made in advance. Spread in the centre and all over top of cake, flicking up in a dastardly fashion.

Tip: *I now use the spray-on oil for oiling tins (also brilliant on graters before grating cheese) such as non-stick sunflower oil cooking spray, about £2.*

This recipe is from a very great friend who professes to be no cook but invariably produces – as if from nowhere – exquisite and imaginative meals. By vocation Diana is a musician, and musicians are usually very methodical: I can see why she enjoys the original measuring system used here.

If this cake becomes part of your regular baking schedule, vary it by using lemon instead of orange (same quantities throughout).

1. Preheat the oven to 170°C/fan oven 150°C/gas 3. Line a loaf tin of 1 litre/1¾-pint capacity with greased greaseproof or baking paper.
2. Put all the cake ingredients in a bowl or food mixer with a pinch of salt and mix thoroughly. Bake for 1 hour until nice and brown on top. If using a fan oven, use the same temperature but watch carefully from 50 minutes onwards as it browns very quickly.
3. Meanwhile, heat the orange juice with the sugar until dissolved. Turn the cake out of its tin and while still warm brush the top repeatedly with the glaze until all is absorbed and the top slightly crunchy.

Tip: *Save odd scraps of greaseproof or baking paper, and when grating citrus rind, simply place a strip over the grating area before grating. The paper will stick to the grater and stop all the lovely zest getting caught in between the protrusions. When finished, simply scrape the zest from the paper into your cake mixture of whatever. Easier to wash up, too.*

Diana's orange yogurt cake

- Dead easy
- Preparation just 15 minutes
- About 1 hour in the oven
Slices into 10
- Keeps 3 or 4 days and freezes well

150ml/5fl oz tub of plain low-fat yogurt (use the tub as a measure for the rest of the ingredients)
2 tubs of self-raising flour
½ tsp baking powder
1½ tubs of caster sugar
½ tub of oil, such as sunflower
2 eggs
grated rind of one orange
pinch of salt

For the Glaze
juice of ½ orange
2 tbsp sugar

Maximise on your citrus zest by slipping a piece of baking paper between fruit and grater.

Fuller's was one of the great British tearooms, from the same inter and post-war stable as Lyons and Kardomah, and later Ceylon Tea Houses.

Cakes and bakes

Fuller's walnut cake

- Worth the effort
- 20 minutes to prepare
- 40 minutes baking, 20 minutes for the icing

Cuts into 6

100g/4oz walnut halves
200g/8oz butter
200g/8oz caster sugar
1 tsp vanilla extract
3 eggs
200g/8oz plain flour
1 tsp baking powder

For the Buttercream
85g/3oz unsalted butter
110g/4oz icing sugar
½ tsp vanilla extract

For the Icing
1 egg white
pinch of cream of tartar
225g/8oz caster sugar
few drops of vanilla extract

1. Line the bottoms of two or three 15cm/6-inch sandwich or cake tins (ideally, or use two 18cm/7-inch tins) with baking parchment. Heat the oven to 160°C/fan oven 140°C/gas 3. Set aside the seven finest walnut halves and chop the rest finely. Cream the butter and sugar with the vanilla and beat in the eggs. Fold in the flour sifted with the baking powder and then the remaining nuts. Pile into the tins and use a spoon to smooth the top, making a deep indentation as the mixture will rise and you want a level surface. Bake for 40 minutes (35 minutes in a fan oven) – in each case 5 minutes less if using the larger tin size – then remove from the oven and cool on racks.

2. Whip the butter, icing sugar and vanilla to a cream. Sandwich the cakes together generously and using a knife, smooth over the sides (not top).

3. Beat the egg white until stiff. Dissolve the cream of tartar in 1 tsp water. Dissolve the caster sugar in 4 tbsp water. When boiling, add the cream of tartar. Boil vigorously until – sooner than you think – a little of the syrup dropped in water can be gathered into a ball (softball – 240°F on a sugar thermometer). Pour in a thin stream over the egg white, beating all the time. Continue beating and when the mixture starts to cool and thicken, spread over the top and down the sides of cake. It will form a light crust.

Tip: *I do prefer the halved walnuts you can buy to walnut pieces – they look crisper and fresher and make a real difference to a cake like this.*

A classic cake with a history

I love breadmaking, and here is my classic recipe for hot cross buns.

Nothing can touch a home-made hot cross bun

1. If using fresh yeast, dissolve it in the milk with the sugar before mixing with all the other ingredients. Otherwise, put all of the first set of ingredients in your biggest bowl and make a dough. Knead for 10 minutes, or 3 minutes in a food mixer with a dough hook. Cover the bowl with a tea towel and leave to rise for 1–1½ hours till doubled in volume.

2. Knock down and knead again for 3 minutes (1 minute with a dough hook). Grease two baking sheets (I do this with that new spray-on oil intended for light frying) and divide the mixture into 13. Roll them very thoroughly into bun shapes (otherwise they will not stay neat while cooking) and put on the trays to rise again for 30 minutes. Preheat the oven to 190°C/fan oven 170°C/gas 5.

3. Make almond-flavoured crosses by rubbing the butter into the flour and working in the sugar, almond essence and 1 tsp water. Roll out thinly. Cut into strips, dampen and stick onto the now-risen buns, cutting the ends of the strips at an angle as you would ribbon. Bake for 20 minutes.

4. Remove from the oven to a rack. For the glaze, dissolve the sugar in milk and brush each bun twice.

Tip 1: *Spelt flour is a wonderful speciality flour that improves taste and texture. You can find it in health shops and some supermarkets.*

Tip 2: *Citrus slices, sold in 50g/2oz packs, look like orange and lemon slices in syrup and give a lovely peel flavour without too much bitterness.*

Hot cross buns

- Easy
- 30 minutes active work
- 2 hours rising, 20 minutes baking

Makes: a baker's dozen
- Open-freeze then put in freezer bags if making ahead

25g/1oz fresh yeast, or 7g sachet fast-action dried yeast
250ml/9fl oz milk and water mixed, at blood heat
50g/2oz muscovado sugar
1 tsp salt
3 tsp mixed spice
50g/2oz butter
500g/1lb 2oz strong white flour (or, if you can get it, 150g/6oz spelt flour, 350g/12oz strong white – see tip)
100g/4oz dried fruit of your choice – including chopped citrus slices if you enjoy peel (see tip)
1 egg

For the Crosses
25g/1oz butter
50g/2oz flour
1 tsp sugar
a little almond essence

For the Glaze
3 tbsp sugar
1 tbsp milk

I had this recipe for years, without ever knowing who or what Fochabers might be. My resourceful mother had a hunch it might be Scottish and found it in an atlas: our thanks to this small town on the River Spey in Grampian for producing such a very fine gingerbread.

It isn't too black and treacly, and is enriched by ground almonds and fruit. A tip: it improves if kept for a couple of days before baking.

Fochabers gingerbread

Cakes and bakes

- Simple, honest baking
- 30 minutes to prepare
- 1½ hours to bake
Cuts into 10
- Keeps for a week

100g/4oz butter
100g/4oz sugar
100g/4oz black treacle, slightly warmed
1 egg
½ tsp bicarbonate of soda
150ml/¼ pint beer
250g/9oz flour
50g/2oz sultanas
50g/2oz currants
35g/1½oz ground almonds
35g/1½oz chopped peel
2 tsp mixed spice
2 tsp ground ginger
½ tsp cinnamon
¼ tsp ground cloves

1. Preheat the oven to 150°C/fan oven 130°C/gas 2. Take a loaf tin of 850ml/1½ pint capacity and line the bottom and sides with baking parchment.

2. Cream the butter well with sugar and treacle (warming makes it easier to measure). Beat in the egg.

3. Measure the bicarbonate into the beer and stir to dissolve.

4. Meanwhile, mix the flour with all the remaining ingredients and beat into the creamed mixture.

5. Give the beer mixture a final stir and beat into the creamed mixture thoroughly. Transfer into the tin, smooth the top and knock the tin sharply on the work surface to settle the contents.

6. Bake for 1½ hours in the centre of the oven. A skewer will come out clean when cooked. Leave to cool in the tin in the wrappings, then when cold wrap again in plastic film and store in an airtight tin. Matures well.

Tip: *Always measure bicarbonate of soda very accurately, and don't imagine adding more will lighten a cake – it may well cause it to collapse. It is usually added to a liquid and dissolved before incorporating in a cake mixture, unlike baking powder, which is added to the dry ingredients.*

A fine rich gingerbread from northern Scotland

A lovely light American cake with a wonderful flavour that my mother has been making since the year I was born.

Even marginal differences in your oven thermostat will make a difference when you're baking for as long as 2¼ hours. I advise testing the cake 10 minutes before the end of cooking and continuing doing so every 10 minutes until the skewer comes out clean.

1. Rinse the currants to remove any grit, pick out any foreign bodies and dry on kitchen paper; this can be done the day before. Preheat oven to 160°C/fan oven 140°C/gas 3. Line a deep 20cm/8-inch loose-bottomed cake tin with greased greaseproof or baking paper.
2. Cream the butter with the sugar until soft. Beat in the eggs one at a time and the flour. Add the currants, and the cherries. Add the citron peel, grate in the nutmeg and add the whisky. Mix thoroughly and turn into the tin. Flatten the mixture with a spatula and tap the tin sharply on a work surface to settle the contents. Then make a smooth 2.5cm/1-inch depression in the centre of the mixture, sloping up to the sides.
3. Bake for 1 hour, cover loosely with foil and bake for a further 1 hour 15 minutes until nicely browned and the cake has all but stopped singing. A hot skewer inserted in the centre should come out clean. Leave in the tin to cool for 1 hour, then turn out but leave the paper on. When absolutely cold, remove the wrappings, rewrap in clingfilm and keep in a tin.

Tip: *I prefer the colour and flavour of the darker red glacé cherries sold as undyed or naturally coloured – try them if you can find them.*

Make a deep concave dip in the top of the cake to ensure a flat top once baked.

Light cherry christmas cake

- Quite simple
- 30 minutes preparation
- 2¼ hours baking
Makes a 20cm/8-inch cake

500g/1lb 2oz currants
250g/9oz butter
200g/8oz caster sugar
4 eggs (they must be large)
200g/8oz plain flour
200g/8oz glacé cherries (see tip), diced
100g/4oz mixed citron peel, finely chopped
½ nutmeg
2 tbsp whisky

Shortbread topped with a gooey caramel mixture, drizzled with chocolate: sounds almost too good for children, doesn't it? Nevertheless, Meriel Greenwood of Crook, near Kendal in Cumbria, wrote to me and told me her grandchildren Karina, Laurie and Christie think it is fantastic, and I do too.

The caramel is made by boiling condensed milk – the sweetened kind that comes in tins and looks and tastes like melted white chocolate. The only other time I have used this rather sickly product is to make Banoffee Pie (the gooey dessert created by the Hungry Monk restaurant in Sussex). In that recipe you boil the tin without opening in a pan of water for 2 hours (if you ever do this – and the manufacturers don't recommend it – you must let the tin cool fully before opening). Alternatively, if you can find a new caramel milk product in jars called Dulce de Leche, by Merchant Gourmet, use half a jar of that.

Meriel's marvels

Cakes and bakes

- Easy
- 20 minutes to prepare
- 15 minutes to cook

Makes: 24 irresistible marvels

For the Shortbread
100g/4oz butter – unsalted if feeling lavish
60g/2oz golden caster sugar
175g/6oz plain flour
pinch of salt

For the Caramel
100g/4oz butter
3 tbsp golden syrup
small (218g) tin sweetened condensed milk (not evaporated)

For the Topping
100g/4oz bar of good quality plain chocolate

1. Preheat the oven to 180°C/fan oven 160°C/gas 4. Make the shortbread by creaming the butter with the sugar, then stirring in the flour with a pinch of salt. Keep stirring and the mixture will gradually form into one mass rather than crumbs, knead lightly, shape into a fat sausage and put directly on to an ungreased baking sheet. Use a rolling pin to roll out thinly to about 20 × 28cm/8 × 11 inches – keep the edges straight and neat by patting into shape between rollings. No need to flour the rolling pin, though it is easier with a little.

2. Bake for 13–15 minutes, till golden. Cool on the tray for 2 minutes, slide a palette knife under to loosen, then carefully slide on to a board.

3. You can make the caramel while the base is cooking or later. Put the butter, syrup and milk in a deep pan. Bring to the boil slowly and boil, stirring, for 5–6

minutes, until it darkens in colour and you can smell caramel. Allow to cool, then spread on to the shortbread.

4. Melt the chocolate and drizzle over in a criss-cross fashion. Cut into small squares and enjoy.

Tip 1: *Few things annoy me more than recipes that call for unsalted butter as if it's the norm. It's more expensive, and most people have salted in their fridge, so why? The only times I use it are for spreading on bread (which is pure personal preference) and in recipes that actually taste of butter – shortbread is undeniably one of these. Unsalted has a finer flavour, but this is only significant if you can actually taste it in the finished dish.*

Tip 2: *If you won the lottery last night you may wish to press a layer of chopped toasted nuts and raisins on to the caramel before drizzling with the chocolate.*

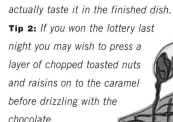

Meriel's secret shared with the world

This recipe was gleaned from a woman whose house we were buying, and who served it over a conversation about curtains, carpets and light fittings. They say that if you want to sell a house you should fill it with the aroma of baking bread, vanilla and freshly ground coffee – but this is what worked for Mrs Robinson.

Mrs Robinson's madeira cake

- No trouble
- 20 minutes preparation
- 1–1¼ hours baking
Cuts into 8
- Keeps for up to a week in a tin and can be frozen

160g/6oz soft margarine such as Blue Band, or butter (see tip)
190g/7oz caster sugar
¼ tsp vanilla extract
3 large eggs, separated
225g/8oz self-raising flour
150g carton of natural yogurt
1 tbsp caraway seeds, optional
a little caster sugar

1. Heat the oven to 170°C/fan oven 150°C/gas 3. Grease an 18cm/7-inch cake tin and line the base with a disc of greased greaseproof paper.

2. Cream the margarine or butter with the sugar and vanilla and beat in the egg yolks. Divide the flour and yogurt each into three batches and mix them alternately into the creamed mixture till well combined. (If using caraway seeds, add them with last batch of flour.)

3. Beat the egg whites till stiff but not dry. Using a metal spoon and figure-of-eight motion, thoroughly fold a good dollop of whites into the creamed mixture to loosen it, then fold in the rest.

4. Turn into the tin and bake in the centre of the oven for 1–1¼ hours, until a knife inserted in the centre comes out clean. Cover with foil after 45 minutes if necessary to prevent it becoming too brown; the cake will rise in the centre and may crack but this is correct and it will sink after a little cooling. Serve dredged with caster sugar.

A truly seductive cake

Tip: *I am not a great advocate of margarine, but having made this with both soft margarine and butter, I have found that margarine unquestionably gives a lighter, softer result, as well as being extremely easy to use.*

An urban myth was travelling round the cookery circuit concerning cookies served up in the café of the most swanky department store in Texas, Neiman Marcus. The story went that a woman and her daughter (one's imagination conjures up Dallas-style blondes a-glitter with rhinestones) liked the cookies so much they asked if they might have the recipe, to be told it would be "two-fifty".

A month later the mother's credit card statement (platinum card, no doubt) comes in, listing "Cookie recipe – $250". To get even, the woman decided to have $250-worth of fun spreading the recipe round the world.

1. Preheat oven to 180°C/fan oven 160°C/gas 4. Line two large baking sheets with baking parchment. Whizz the oats in a processor until finely ground. Add flour, bicarbonate of soda and salt and whizz again to mix.
2. In another mixer or by hand, cream the butter with sugars; beat in the egg and vanilla, then stir in all the remaining ingredients, including the oat-flour mixture, until well combined.
3. Form into about 16 golf-ball size balls and put on the baking sheets, allowing as much distance in between as possible. Bake for 15–17 minutes, switching the position of the trays after 5 minutes. Cool for a minute on the tray then transfer to a cooling rack with a spatula. These cookies are deliciously crisp around the edge with soft centres.

Tip: *The better the chocolate the better the flavour.*

Scrumptious millionaire-style cookies

The $250 cookie

● Easy and fun to make
● 20 minutes to mix
● 15–17 minutes in the oven
Makes 16 large deluxe cookies

85g/3oz rolled oats
100g/4oz self-raising flour
½ tsp bicarbonate of soda
½ tsp salt
100g/4oz butter
50g/2oz soft brown sugar
50g/2oz demerara sugar
1 large egg
½ tsp vanilla extract
25g/1oz desiccated coconut
200g/8oz plain chocolate, chopped
85g/3oz walnuts, chopped

These wonderful biscuits are remarkable because the white chocolate taste is so powerful – usually it is rather an indeterminate flavour. The vanilla brings it out, and as ever I recommend readers to seek out vanilla extract rather than the synthetic essence. You can get it nowadays at good supermarkets and delicatessens, or by mail order from Lakeland, Alexandra Buildings, Windermere, Cumbria LA23 1BQ.

As someone who eats as few artificial flavourings as possible, I always notice when I stumble across them, wherever that may be. Many years ago I went to a dinner party that was course after course of supermarket ready-made dishes, and though I admired the brazenness, it was a nightmare of overseasoning and artificially-boosted tastiness.

White chocolate and vanilla crunches

Cakes and bakes

- Quick and easy
- 20 minutes to mix
- 12–15 minutes baking
Makes: 18
- They keep well in a tin

50g/2oz good quality white chocolate
140g/5oz self-raising flour
100g/4oz butter, softened to room temperature
50g/2oz caster sugar
few drops of vanilla extract

1. Preheat the oven to 180°C/fan oven 160°C/gas 4. Chop the chocolate finely. Pile all the ingredients into a bowl and mix vigorously till all is well combined.
2. Shape the mixture into 18 balls the size of a walnut and put on two ungreased baking sheets. Using a fork dipped in water each time, flatten out each ball.
3. Bake for 12–15 minutes (the shorter time for a fan oven) until firm and golden – do not overbake, as the biscuits will crisp as they cool. Transfer after a minute to a wire rack.

Tip: *With all-in-one methods such as this, it is paramount that the butter is completely soft. If not, cream the butter with sugar and vanilla first and then mix in the flour and chocolate.*

A scrumptious home-bake for teatime – or anytime

Food for friends

This chapter contains special recipes suitable for buffets, more formal entertaining and larger numbers of guests. Most can be doubled in quantity or you can make several of the same thing to feed a crowd. Though not necessarily difficult or complicated to make, the dishes benefit from a little finesse in the presentation, so that guests can eat with their eyes before they actually get to tuck in.

This iced dessert was invented by the Savoy for a luncheon to celebrate the (first) wedding of HRH Princess Anne; it was cut from a newspaper (very probably *The Express*) by my mother, who has been serving it to acclaim ever since.

As you can see, it is a simple folding-together of whipped cream and meringue with some delectable flavourings. It is something of a special occasion dish, so put it in the freezer when you've an hour or two to spare and unleash it when you want to impress.

Bombe Princess Anne

- Easy
- 15 minutes to prepare
- 2 hours to bake the meringues, otherwise no cooking, 4 hours freezing
Serves: 6–8
- Make in advance

3 egg whites
85g/3oz caster sugar
4 pieces of stem ginger (the kind that comes in a jar with syrup)
425ml/¾ pint double cream
grated rind of a lemon
3 tbsp kirsch
2 tbsp caster sugar

1. To make the meringues, whisk the egg whites till stiff, add half the sugar and beat for 1 minute. Fold in the rest of the sugar with a fork (if you have a metal mixing bowl get a friend to hold his or her hands over your ears as it does make a shocking noise). Line a baking sheet with baking paper. Put 6 mounds of meringue on the baking sheet and bake for 2 hours at 150°C/fan oven 130°C/gas 2. Cool.
2. Line a shallow 18cm/7-inch cake tin with plastic film. Chop the ginger finely. Whisk the cream till just stiff but not dry and fold in the remaining ingredients plus the meringues, roughly broken up (don't overdo this). Pile into the tin and freeze for four hours or longer, turn out ten minutes before serving and cut in slices like a cake. Good with fruit salad.

A recipe with the royal touch

Tip 1: *You could cheat and buy meringues, in which case you'll need about 6 bun-sized meringues, or the equivalent.*

Tip 2: *Iced desserts, and home-made ice cream (especially fruit flavours), do not keep their flavour indefinitely in the freezer. After 2 weeks I find they start to get a bit tasteless.*

These are simply the best cheese biscuits you can ever serve at a drinks party. It took me many moons to pluck up courage to ask my neighbour Susan Gough (a fabulous cook) what the secret was, but she was most generous with her wisdom.

The biscuits appear to have an attractive shiny glaze on them – this is the egg.

1. Grease 3 baking sheets. Preheat the oven to 190°C/fan oven 170°C/gas 5. Sift the flour into a bowl and rub in the butter, then work in the cheddar, cayenne, salt and pepper. No liquid is necessary. If you have a processor, pile everything in (butter must be at room temperature) and whizz with 1 tbsp water to bind (see tip).
2. Roll out as thinly as you can (about 3mm if you are in measuring mood) on a lightly floured surface and cut into 8cm/3-inch rounds with a fluted cutter. Put these on the baking sheets and brush all over the surface with beaten egg (but not down the sides). Bake for 9–10 minutes – though most biscuits are best cooked till just pale, these are better on the golden side.
3. Cool for a minute or two and transfer carefully to racks to cool.

Tip 1: *To transfer the uncooked biscuits to the baking sheets, use a slice or they will break up or stretch.*
Tip 2: *If you make pastry or biscuit dough by hand you will find the heat of your hands warms the ingredients slightly, which helps to bind them. Therefore if you make by machine a little extra water is often necessary.*

An ultra-sophisticated nibble to serve with drinks

Cheese sablés

- Easy
- 15 minutes to prepare
- 9–10 minutes baking

Makes: 36 biscuits

- They keep well in a tin but are very fragile

100g/4oz flour
100g/4oz butter
100g/4oz grated cheddar
a little cayenne
beaten egg
salt and pepper

This is a lovely recipe for a relaxed summer lunch party – perfect for making ahead, and the flavours and appearance are delightful.

Chicken, orange and banana salad

- No special skills required
- 30 minutes to prepare
- 15 minutes' cooking

Serves: 8

140g/5oz long-grain rice
450g/1lb cooked, boned
    chicken (4 small chicken
    breasts)
4 large oranges
2 bananas
4 egg yolks (see tip)
400ml/14fl oz lightly flavoured
    oil – such as sunflower oil
50g/2oz blanched almonds,
    halved, or flaked almonds
salad leaves
a little vinaigrette dressing
    (if making up specially,
    use 2 tsp wine vinegar,
    4 tbsp oil, 1 tsp mustard
    and seasoning, whisked
    together)
small bunch of parsley,
    chopped finely
salt and freshly ground pepper

1. Cook the rice in plenty of boiling salted water for 12–15 minutes until cooked as you like it. (The craze for "al dente" cooking is all very well, but pasta, potatoes and rice simply don't taste very nice unless they are tender.) Drain and leave in the colander.

2. Cut the chicken into strips and put in a large shallow bowl. Grate the rind from one orange and put in a medium bowl. Cut the skin and pith off the oranges and either segment (leaving the membranes behind) with a just-sharpened knife, or cut into slices, discarding the pips. Catch the juices and add 4 tbsp (no more) to the rind, set aside. Add the orange segments to the chicken, then slice the bananas into thin oblique slices and add to the bowl; mix everything together with your hands so the banana gets coated with juice.

3. Make the mayonnaise by putting the egg yolks with the orange rind and juice and stirring together. Pour in the oil drop by drop, stirring to make an emulsion, then stir more vigorously. The orange juice will mean that it will not be as stiff as regular mayonnaise. Season to taste. Finally, toast the halved almonds in a pan or under the grill until golden – 3–5 minutes only.

4. The finesse of this dish is in its assembly. Moisten the salad leaves with some of the vinaigrette and arrange on a serving dish. Mix the rice with half the orange-banana-chicken mixture and some vinaigrette to moisten. Pile on to the salad leaves. Fold enough mayonnaise into the remaining chicken mixture to moisten, then arrange over the rice and chicken mixture. Just before serving, drizzle over extra mayonnaise and top with the almonds and parsley.

Tip 1: *If you don't want to make your own mayonnaise, stir 2 tbsp orange juice into 600ml/1 pint Hellmann's or other good make of mayonnaise (not low-fat).*

Tip 2: *Some cooks are plagued by sticky rice. I blame those elaborate methods whereby you measure the water and rice by volume and cook until the former is entirely absorbed – a treacherous fiddle, I find. The best way is to boil up loads of water, add the rice and when it is cooked, drain well. Stir occasionally as it cools, but no need to rinse.*

Slice the banana like this

Dark treacle and cinnamon parfait

- Surprisingly easy
- 30 minutes to prepare and cook

Serves: 6

- Make the day before

564ml carton of whipping cream
3 medium eggs, separated
4 tbsp black treacle
2 tsp cinnamon
175g/6oz icing sugar
pinch of salt

This is a gem of a recipe and the perfect creative dessert for a dinner party since it is all prepared ahead. It comes from the kitchen of someone who often sends me recipes, and whose tastebuds seem to be perfectly aligned with mine: Patricia Gregory of Prestbury near Cheltenham (see also Custard cuddles on page 100).

The flavour is intense and slightly spicy. It's a doddle to make – and is sure to intrigue and impress guests. Be aware however that it contains uncooked eggs.

1. Put a 1.2 litre/2-pint metal mould or cake tin in the freezer. Lightly whip the cream and add the yolks, treacle and cinnamon; sift in the icing sugar and whip to soft peaks.

2. In a separate bowl, whisk the egg whites with a pinch of salt until stiff. Fold the two mixtures together. Slip into the mould and freeze for 12 hours. Remove to fridge 20 minutes before serving to soften a little.

This can be served as you would an ice-cream, scooped, or turned out. Good with biscuits.

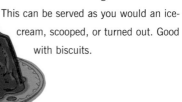

A luscious frozen dessert for autumn

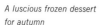

This is one of my mother's favourite puddings, and it is great fun to make at home. One piece of special equipment will help enormously: a mouli food mill (fitted with the medium disc) or potato ricer, to extrude the chestnut mixture in thin, rice-like pieces, which gives the correct texture.

Food as art – a mountain of meringue, chestnut and whipped cream

Mont blanc

Food for friends

1. For the meringue, preheat the oven to 110°C/fan oven 90°C/gas ¼. Draw a 20cm/8-inch circle on baking parchment and put on a baking sheet. Whisk egg whites till very stiff and beat in ¾ of the sugar until at the stiff peak stage. Fold in the remaining sugar, hazelnuts and cornflour. Spoon on to the circle on the baking sheet and bake until crisp, 1½–2 hours. Remove from the paper with a palette knife and if still soft underneath return to oven to crisp.

2. Drain the chestnuts and put through the mouli (or sieve). Dissolve the sugar in the water and boil vigorously for 5 minutes. Beat the chestnuts and vanilla into the syrup till smooth.

3. Find a shallow bowl of 20cm/8-inch diameter, so the meringue disc will just fit in the top, like a lid. Line the bottom of the bowl with baking parchment. Mouli or sieve the chestnut mixture into the bowl so it falls evenly into it – do not fork or smooth the mixture in any way, it is meant to stay light and aerated. Refrigerate.

4. Assemble by putting the meringue over the bowl, then a serving dish over that, and inverting so the chestnut sits elegantly on the meringue base. Cover with a snow-cap of cream, lightly whipped (not too stiff), and sprinkle over the chocolate. Serve in slices, cake-style.

- Worth the effort
- 40 minutes total preparation
- 2 hours baking
Serves: 8
- Meringue and chestnut are made ahead, assemble at the last minute

For the Hazelnut Meringue
2 egg whites
100g/4oz caster sugar
50g/2oz toasted ground
    hazelnuts
1 tsp cornflour

For the Chestnut Mixture
2 × 425g tins chestnuts in
    water (Epicure do them)
100g/4oz sugar
150ml/¼ pint water
½ tsp vanilla extract

To Finish
425ml/¾ pint double or
    whipping cream
a little grated chocolate

This recipe is one local to my part of Oxfordshire where it is known as "Auntie Roe's egg mousse." The auntie in question – not my own – was Countess Orssich. This simple dish has a real grandeur about it, all the virtues of delightfully innocent egg mayonnaise but with much more flavour and charisma.

Old-fashioned egg mousse

Food for friends

- Fun and different
- 40 minutes to prepare
- 1–2 hours setting

Serves: 6

- Make in advance or leave overnight

150ml/¼ pint condensed beef consommé (half a 295g can)
1 tsp powdered gelatine
2 tbsp mango chutney
2 tsp Worcestershire Sauce
2 tsp curry paste
9 hard-boiled eggs
284ml carton of double cream
salt and freshly ground black pepper

1. Take a 1-litre/1¾-pint soufflé or other attractive serving dish. Heat the consommé in a pan and stir in the gelatine until dissolved.

2. Mix the chutney, Worcestershire sauce and curry paste in a small bowl. Shell the eggs and put the yolks to one side. Coarsely chop the egg whites.

3. Whip the cream in a large bowl till just stiff. Put the yolks through a sieve into the cream and fold in lightly, then fold in the chutney mixture, egg whites and half the consommé mixture all at once. Season lightly, turn into the serving bowl and put in fridge. When just set (this takes 1–2 hours), pour the remaining consomme mixture over carefully to create a marbled topping – you may need to very briefly melt the consommé first.

4. Leave till completely set and serve with toast.

Tip 1: *If you can only find normal canned beef consommé, double the gelatine – it will not make a significant difference to the flavour.*

Tip 2: *I'm sure you know this already, but if you cool hard-boiled eggs in a few changes of cold water they don't get that nasty black ring round the yolk.*

The sort of dish a butler would be proud to serve

This is an extremely impressive dish for entertaining. Check you have a baking sheet that's large enough to take the pastry-wrapped fish, and a serving dish that's big enough.

1. Rub the salmon with the orange zest, mint or dill and lots of black pepper. Sandwich the fillets together and leave for 1 hour in a ceramic dish (metallic will react with the juices and give a metallic taste).

2. Squeeze out the spinach thoroughly. Mix in the cream cheese and season well. Heat the butter and fry the onions for 5 minutes until softened. Stir in the prawns.

3. Preheat the oven to 200°C/fan oven 180°C/gas 6. Now assemble the dish. Roll out one of the packs of pastry to a rectangle measuring 38 × 20cm/15 × 8 inches. Put one of the fish fillets, drained, on top, skinned side down. Spread with the spinach and then the prawn mixture, then put the other fillet on top, skinned side up. Trim the pastry leaving 1cm/½-inch all the way round. Brush the edge with beaten egg then put the other piece of pastry on top and trim to fit. Press the edges down well to seal, make a couple of holes on top and brush all over with egg. If you wish, use the pastry trimmings to make a lattice top and brush with egg again. Refrigerate for a short time before cooking, if convenient.

4 Bake for 40–45 minutes, until puffed and golden. Slide onto a large serving dish.

Tip: *Get as much water as possible out of the spinach or it will leak inside the pastry case.*

A masterpiece for a summer lunch party

Salmon en croûte

- A challenge
- Marinate at least 1 hour before baking
- 40 minutes to prepare
- 45 minutes to cook

Serves: 8

1.6–1.8kg/3½–4lb salmon or salmon trout, skinned and filleted
zest and juice of an orange
1 tbsp fresh mint or dill, chopped, or 2 tsp dried
350g/12oz frozen spinach, thawed
100g/4oz Philadelphia cream cheese
25g/1oz butter
8 spring onions, chopped
115g/4oz cooked prawns
2 × 350g packs of puff pastry – preferably ready-rolled
1 egg, beaten
salt and freshly ground black pepper

This recipe, like all the best, dates from the late 1950s. My mother recalls that her local church (in the United States) used to have a monthly pot-luck supper: you said whether you would be taking a salad, main course or pudding, and everyone helped themselves. Such an occasion really tells you what people like, and this went like greased lightning. Serve with a green salad

Scalloped potatoes

- Very easy
- 20 minutes to prepare
- 1¼ hours in the oven
Serves: 4 as an accompaniment
- Easily multiplied

225g/½lb ham
1kg/2lb 4oz large floury potatoes, such as King Edward or Marfona (see tip)
1 onion
25g/1oz flour
300ml/½ pint hot milk
50g/2oz cheddar cheese
25g/1oz breadcrumbs (1 thick slice of bread)
salt and freshly ground black pepper

1. Preheat the oven to 180°C/fan oven 170°C/gas 4. Grease a deep ovenproof dish or casserole with a lid and a capacity of 1.2 litres/2 pints.

2. Cut the ham into bite-size pieces and put in the bottom of the dish. Peel and slice the potatoes thinly, and chop the onion. Layer them up on top of the ham, sprinkling with the flour and seasoning as you go. Finish with a layer of potatoes.

3. Pour over the just-boiled milk, then grate over the cheese and finish with the breadcrumbs. Stand the dish on a baking tray in case it boils over.

4. Bake for 30 minutes covered, then remove the lid and cook for a further 45 minutes, until potatoes are soft and the dish nicely browned.

Tip: *Watch your potatoes! Waxy potatoes simply refuse to cook by this method – they never get tender – so choose large old floury ones such as King Edward or Marfona.*

Sliced ham is topped by a thick layer of potatoes with a crunchy topping

This is a glamorous first course or appetiser – a cousin of the sausage roll, only made with salmon and prawns and no pastry. They're very easy to make, and I promise there will be none leftover.

1. Whip the cream till beginning to thicken and stir in the horseradish and lemon juice, which will complete the stiffening process. Cut up the prawns roughly and stir them in with some seasoning.

2. Lay out all the salmon slices and put a dollop of the mixture on each slice at one of its narrow ends – a good tablespoon per slice. Roll up each neatly towards its other narrow end to make short thick rolls – a sort of sausage roll shape.

3. Chill in the fridge. When ready serve with the lemon quarters and grind black pepper over.

Tip: *To make this recipe into canapés, slice the salmon slices lengthwise to be extra narrow, and put on a good teaspoonful of mixture before rolling. Secure each with a cocktail stick.*

Chill the rolls well and they can be eaten with the fingers

Smoked salmon parcels

- Easy
- No cooking
- A few minutes preparation

Serves: 6 as canapés, 4 as a starter

- Can be prepared up to half a day ahead

142ml carton of double cream or crème fraîche
1 tbsp grated horseradish, or hot horseradish sauce
1 tbsp lemon juice (quarter of a lemon)
125g/4oz pack small prawns
250g/9oz pack smoked salmon slices (8–10 slices)
cocktail sticks, optional (see tip)
lemon quarters, to serve
salt and freshly ground black pepper

Food for friends

This recipe was a special request by reader Pat Holness of Plymouth (if you live in the area, yes it's her, the one with her own radio show). She asked for a warm and comforting casserole that looks after itself, so I hope this fits the bill, at the same time as being interesting and different.

Many people are now eating venison in preference to beef. At about three times the price of stewing steak, venison isn't a cheap option, but cook it like this and it is every bit as tender as beef.

Venison and chestnut casserole

- Easy
- 30 minutes to prepare
- 2¼–2½ hours to cook
Serves: 6
- Freezes well

2 onions
175g/6oz smoked streaky bacon
2 cloves of garlic
2 large potatoes
1kg/2lb 4oz stewing venison, cut into medium cubes
2 tbsp olive oil, plus extra if necessary
200g/8oz cooked chestnuts, vacuum-packed or canned (see tip)
bouquet garni
½ tsp cayenne pepper
300ml/½ pint red wine
300ml/½ pint beef or other stock
salt and freshly ground black pepper

1. Preheat the oven to 150°C/fan oven 130°C/gas 2. First get all the chopping done: chop the onions, de-rind and slice the bacon finely, crush the garlic and peel and halve the potatoes. If using pre-diced venison check it is evenly cut as the people who do this (or is it robots nowadays?) don't seem to be very consistent about this.

2. Now start cooking: everything is first sizzled in the frying pan before transferring to the casserole. So heat half the oil in a large frying pan and fry the onions and bacon for 5 minutes till starting to go golden; add the garlic for another minute. Remove to a comfortable-sized lidded casserole. Now add the remaining oil and fry the venison in two or three batches, keeping the heat high so the venison sizzles and browns: the aim is to get it toasted, rather than just beige, so allow 5–7 minutes. Transfer to the casserole. Fry the chestnuts similarly for 3–4 minutes, using a little more oil to moisten and transfer to the casserole. Bring the remaining ingredients except the potatoes to the boil in the frying pan, scraping up any bits, and transfer to the casserole, then add the potatoes and bring once again to the boil. Season (not too much salt on account of the bacon) before transferring to the oven.

3. Bake for 2 hours 15 minutes, stirring a couple of times (otherwise the pieces of meat on the surface will blacken). At this point, remove the potatoes and a few spoonfuls of the juices to a food processor or liquidiser: whizz till smooth and return to the pan (this will thicken the sauce). Stir in well and put back in the oven till ready to serve. Good accompaniments are mashed potato and cabbage.

Tip 1: *I am very fond of the vacuum-packed chestnuts sold by the company Merchant Gourmet; otherwise use a 240g can of chestnuts.*
Tip 2: *Although this seems a low heat, it cooks the venison to perfection.*

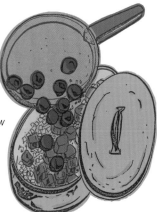

A rich autumn stew

This is a really inventive and unusual first course from a fashionable London restaurant, the Sugar Club in Notting Hill (now renamed Bali Sugar). It was my friend David who first spotted it and started to make it; I have changed the proportions slightly from Peter Gordon's original, and in case you can't get watermelon (it's touch-and-go in the part of Oxfordshire in which I live) I have tried it with normal melon and it's excellent, if less colourful.

Watermelon and pumpkin seed salad

Food for friends

- Very easy
- 15 minutes to prepare
- ½ hour chilling

Serves: 6 as a very glamorous and unusual first course
- Can be prepared up to 1 hour ahead

100g/4oz bag pumpkin seeds
2 tbsp olive oil
200g/8oz feta cheese
1.3kg/3lb watermelon or melon (800g/1¾lb prepared weight)
1 lemon
freshly ground black pepper

1. Preheat the oven to 180°C/fan oven 160°C/gas 4. Put the seeds in a shallow tin with half the oil and toast in the oven till light brown (about 8 minutes), stirring occasionally. Set aside.

2. Cut the cheese into 2cm/¾-inch dice. Make the melon into rough balls if you have a melon baller, or dice. Put in a large salad bowl, add the pumpkin seeds, and the remaining oil.

3. Chill and serve with freshly ground pepper and lemon quarters.

Tip: *Pumpkin seeds are easily obtainable from Holland and Barratt and large supermarkets – not to be confused with sunflower seeds.*

A beautiful tumble of ingredients – the original recipe is said to come from Israel

These celebration truffles make an excellent gift – but do mention they contain fresh ingredients and need to be kept in the fridge. If making more than this amount, do it in batches as the nuts will otherwise fail to melt the chocolate and butter in step 2.

The little logs literally melt in the mouth

White chocolate hazelnut truffles

1. Preheat the oven or grill to hot. Toast the hazelnuts in a tin or ovenproof dish for 5–7 minutes until pale gold – watch carefully.
2. Allow to cool in the tin for 3–4 minutes and then tip into a food processor bowl. Grind thoroughly. Add unsalted butter and chocolate, in pieces, and whizz till smooth and melted: the heat from the hazelnuts will achieve this. Stir or whizz in the brandy and icing sugar.
3. Turn on to a piece of waxed paper on a plate and form with a spoon or spatula into a block about 15cm/6-inches square. Refrigerate for 2 hours.
4. The mixture is ready to mould when it no longer sticks to your finger when pressed; wait for this moment or it will all end in tears. Equip yourself with a board (upon which to mould the truffles) and a plate (upon which to put them when shaped). Sprinkle both with icing sugar. Take a teaspoonful of mixture, put it on the board and with icing-sugared fingers roll delicately into a small log. If the mixture starts to get too soft to handle, rechill it for 10–20 minutes and finish later.
5. Decorate with a light freckling of sifted cocoa and transfer with fingertips to a pretty glass or white plate.

Tip: *These truffles are extremely rich and need to be served straight from the fridge.*

- Requires patience and a light touch, but easy
- 20 minutes preparation
- 2 hours cooling

Makes: 25–30

- Truffles keep a week in the fridge
- Serve chilled with coffee

100g/4oz bag shelled hazelnuts
100g/4oz unsalted butter, at room temperature
100g/4oz bar of high quality white chocolate, such as Lindt, at room temperature
1 tbsp brandy
50g/2oz icing sugar, plus extra for moulding
cocoa